# MOVIES TO MANAGE BY

## LESSONS IN LEADERSHIP FROM GREAT FILMS

JOHN K. CLEMENS
AUTHOR OF *THE CLASSIC TOUCH*
AND MELORA WOLFF

CB

CONTEMPORARY BOOKS

Library of Congress Cataloging-in-Publication Data

Clemens, John, 1939.
    Movies to manage by : lessons in leadership from great films / John K. Clemens and
Melora Wolff.
        p.    cm.
    Includes bibliographical references and index.
    ISBN 0-8092-2798-3 (hardcover) — ISBN 0-8092-2796-7 (paperback)
    1. Motion pictures—United States—Plots, themes, etc.    2. Heroes in motion pictures.
3. Leadership.    I. Title    II. Title: Lessons in leadership from great films.

    PN1993.5.U6C56    1999
    791.43'653—dc21                                                                99-26801
                                                                                          CIP

# Contemporary Books

### A Division of The McGraw·Hill Companies

        6 7 8 9 0    LBM/LBM    1 0 9 8 7 6


ISBN 0-8092-2798-3 (hardcover)
ISBN 0-8092-2796-7 (paperback)

This book was set in Adobe Garamond
Printed and bound by Lake Book Manufacturing

Cover design by Kim Bartko
Cover illustration copyright © William Bramhall
Interior design by Jeanette Wojtyla

McGraw-Hill books are available at special quantity discounts to use as premiums and sales promotions, or for use in corporate training programs. For more information, please write to the Director of Special Sales, Professional Publishing, McGraw-Hill, Two Penn Plaza, New York, NY 10121-2298. Or contact your local bookstore.

This book is printed on acid-free paper.

To Karyl and to Lloyd DeBoer

*Also by John K. Clemens*

# THE CLASSIC TOUCH
## Lessons in Leadership from Homer to Hemingway

(with Douglas F. Mayer)

# THE TIMELESS LEADER

(with Steve Albrecht)

# CONTENTS

# ACKNOWLEDGMENTS

We want to acknowledge, first and foremost, the marvelously creative and sensitive artists who wrote, directed, produced, and acted in the films we discuss in this book. We are indebted, too, to the characters they created—both real and imagined—who populate the unforgettable cinematic stories on which *Movies to Manage By* is based.

We would also like to express our appreciation to those who have shared our commitment to bringing the leadership lessons latent in great films to those who manage and lead in today's organizations. First to Dr. Richard A. Detweiler, president of Hartwick College, whose encouragement has been substantial—he has managed to make Hartwick an exciting and creative place to teach. Second, to Dr. Susan D. Gotsch, vice president and dean of academic affairs at Hartwick College, whose administrative savvy and knowledge of the sociology of labor has provided a beacon of light for the project. And, third, to Stephen Kolenda, chair of Hartwick's management department, whose ability to schedule our time adroitly has made this effort possible.

To George, for so much, thanks and love.

Thanks also to Ellen Damsky. *Thank you* to Pangea Farm, for turning the tide. And to Evegeniy Krasnov and Megan McConnelee, two extraordinary students from whom we have learned much.

We also want to thank the Hartwick Humanities in Management Institute's case writers, whose extensive research has yielded a superb library of cases on leadership based on film: Associate Professor of Liberal Arts Christine Jackson of Nova Southeastern University; Associate Professor of Management Stanton Maloney of the University of New England; Gerald McCarthy, Managing Director of OLV Associates in Worcester, Massachusetts; Associate Professor of Management Edward Ottensmeyer of the Graduate School of Business at Clark University; Professor of Philosophy Michael K. Green of the State University of New York at Oneonta; Professor of Management Barry Armandi of the State University of New York at Old Westbury; Professor of History/Political Science James Robinson of the State University of New York, Empire State College; Assistant Professor of American Studies and English Thomas Edwards of Westbrook College; Associate Professor of Management Claudia Harris of North Carolina Central University; Professor of English William Brown of Philadelphia College of Textiles and Science; and Dr. Richard K. Insinga, lecturer in management at the State University of New York at Oneonta.

We want to especially thank our editor, Matthew Carnicelli, who has been a superb alter ego in this endeavor. It was

Matthew's vision that helped create *Movies to Manage By* initially, and his perseverance that kept it going. And our literary agent, Carol Mann, deserves our continuing gratitude for marshaling our books through daunting commercial and creative landscapes. Our project editor at NTC/Contemporary Publishing Group, Nicole Adams, helped to make this a smooth process, and Jackie Blakley's copyediting was superb.

Finally, we are extremely grateful to the W. K. Kellogg Foundation, whose generous grant to the Hartwick Humanities in Management Institute has made this entire project possible.

# Introduction

There is something about film that goes beyond its capacity to entertain. A good movie can also teach. This is particularly true when it comes to managing and leading. While conducting hundreds of leadership seminars for Fortune 500 companies over the past ten years, we've noticed something undeniable. Participants can learn as much (if not more) about effective management and leadership from good movies as they can from traditional books, lectures, or case studies. This book's purpose is to demonstrate that movies can go beyond entertainment to help you to become a more effective leader.

Good films teach significant truths about the human condition, revealing how people think, how they act, and how they dream. And what could be more important to a leader—and to leadership—than honing a greater understanding of what makes people tick? This may require a bit more rigorous approach to film viewing—we call it *purposeful viewing*—but, trust us, you'll still be entertained. And we promise you the benefit will be worth the cost.

Thus, in this book, the film becomes a text that we have endeavored to translate, as best we can, into the language of leadership. We invite you to interpret the films with us in the context of the management and leadership issues they portray, the same issues you face every day. We hope you'll imagine yourself as an actor in the film and see yourself in the leading role. You'll soon discover that this medium is a powerful learning tool.

These movies will change the way you manage and lead. And this book will change the way you watch movies.

Great films, of course, will continue to thrill you, entertain you, amuse you, or make you cry, as they have since the first flickering black-and-white images were crudely projected onto Edison's screen in 1889. But they also have a very practical application for you.

Some of the movies we have chosen for this book illustrate particular skills and practical talents that are vital to good management and leadership. As we developed our list of useful films, we discovered that mere illustration—a "Do this to lead well!" manual—is not enough, and that a guidebook on leadership skills would actually betray some crucial truths about leadership. Good leaders are not born from the study of a well-planned tip sheet, but from an exciting alchemy of qualities that have been stirred to the surface of consciousness by questions, dilemmas, and stories. So you'll discover that *Movies to Manage By* addresses both practical issues (in its opening chapters) and (in its final chapters) more complex matters of morality, values, self-awareness, self- and group inquiry, and dilemmas of character and judgment as revealed by the films.

Examples of practical knowledge for leadership are available, for instance, in *Apollo 13*, the story of NASA's most successful failure. This movie, based on the true story of human ingenuity in a race against technology gone awry, not only entertains but also reveals how stretch goals, remarkable teamwork, and improvisation can turn failure into success in any organization. The film *Norma Rae* shows how a female millworker empowers herself and others, as well as proving how valuable reverse mentoring can be. *Hoosiers* tells the story of a down-and-out basketball coach who turns a failing team into winners in ways that will surprise you.

But leadership is not solely about practice and technique. It also depends on the much more complex qualities of insight, compassion, moral perception, values, and emotional balance. You'll discover, for example, that the movie *Dead Poets Society*—a film about an extraordinary high school English teacher—raises challenging questions about the distinctions between heroism and leadership; and *Wall Street*, though providing few examples of sound leadership, challenges you to draw your own conclusions about moral behavior. The film *Twelve O'Clock High* reminds you of the important truth that sometimes even noble efforts result in a failure of leadership. *Citizen Kane* provides an archetypal tale of a successful leader—he actually writes cinema's first mission statement!—who ultimately fails in life and in leadership because of his all-consuming need for personal power and control over others.

We were disappointed that our research—and a great deal of film viewing—did not produce a satisfactory number of films focusing on women as leaders. We were unwilling to include any of the many films that suggest that a woman's success or failure as a leader is shaped by sexual stereotype. You won't find here a movie about a poor martyr, a domestic nurturer, a genius lunatic, a female Rambo, a good mom, a sexy bully, a man's student, a wretched loner, a willful hysteric, or a desperate survivor. *Norma Rae*, while the story of a female protégé of a male mentor, tells an important leadership story, since the characters establish an equal balance that transcends cliché.

We give you here films that we believe make points about successful and unsuccessful leadership that apply to both women and men. We are glad to report that all of the movies in *Movies to Manage By* affected and inspired us both.

We're sure they'll do the same for you.

# PART ONE

# GUIDING THE SHIP

*Captain Marko Ramius (Sean Connery) transforms a hunch into action in* The Hunt for Red October.

# ONE

# FOLLOWING YOUR HUNCH

## The Hunt for Red October

### CAST OF CHARACTERS

Captain Marko Ramius *(Sean Connery)*

Jack Ryan *(Alec Baldwin)*

Captain Bart Mancuso *(Scott Glenn)*

Captain Vasily Borodin *(Sam Neill)*

Admiral James Greer *(James Earl Jones)*

Seaman Jones *(Courtney B. Vance)*

Jeffrey Pelt *(Richard Jordan)*

Director: John McTiernan

Screenwriters: Larry Ferguson and Donald Stewart

No amount of bobbing around on the surface of a lake or an ocean can prepare you fully for what happens deep in the Atlantic in the Cold War thriller *The Hunt for Red October* (1990). In one of the most riveting scenes in the movie, a submarine as big as a World War II aircraft carrier soars 800 feet beneath the surface, her diving planes extended like the wings of a huge glider. The low vibratory hum of its engines—something between a sound and a flow—belies their awesome power. There are no windows, and no direct sense of the world outside. Yet, traveling at almost 60 miles per hour in this silent, near-virtual environment, *Red October* banks gracefully, first to starboard and then to port, just missing the underwater peaks on either side. Amazingly, aboard this ultra-high-tech war machine packed with computers and guided missiles and nuclear reactors, these perfectly executed maneuvers are made possible by two low-tech and rather ancient devices: a clock and a sailing chart.

This is dead reckoning at its best. Start from a known position, combine the factors of speed and time to solve for distance, and—assuming that vagaries like temperature are amicable—you can fly an airplane through the Grand Canyon with your eyes closed. No hunches here, just hard science.

The submarine's navigator, after checking his stopwatch, casually announces that the next turn in this underwater abyss will come in precisely 6 minutes, 30 seconds. All of this begins to seem almost routine until several minutes later, when a half-ton torpedo acquires the submarine and unrelentingly homes in. The crew's attempts to confuse the torpedo work briefly, but it soon reacquires the submarine and rushes onward, a shark sensing blood. There seems to be no escape for the sub, no room to maneuver. Trying to outrun its pursuer, it is trapped between two jagged cliffs.

The only hope is to make the turn before the steadily gaining torpedo hits. The navigator urgently begins his countdown.

"Four . . . three . . . two . . . one . . . mark!"

Yet the submarine captain does nothing.

"The turn, Captain!" The navigator's voice is urgent.

An underwater Matterhorn looms dead ahead, a collision imminent. Yet the captain seems not to care. He is somewhere else.

"Captain, we are out of the lane!" the navigator exclaims.

But the captain is not listening. Apart from a slight change in his breathing, he shows no particular emotion. His lips move almost imperceptibly, as if he is talking to himself. He's processing information, that is clear.

But he is also "seeing" something that no one else sees.

Finally, just milliseconds before the submarine collides with the escarpment, the captain shouts, "Right full rudder! Reverse starboard engine!" The immense submarine shudders as its rudder and right propeller force it into an emergency turn, and it just misses the cliff face by yards. The torpedo, bewildered by the echoes coming off the terrain, explodes mindlessly into the rocks. This captain, it seems, is a very skilled submarine driver.

No wonder. He is first-rank Soviet Navy captain Marko Ramius. Nicknamed the "Vilnius schoolmaster," he has trained most of the Soviet submarine service's officer corps; he is their "top gun." But, more than anything else, he is a consummate player of hunches who also gives singular credence to Peter Drucker's sage observation that leadership is about *performance*. Ramius *performs*, and he succeeds marvelously.

Of course, *The Hunt for Red October* is only one of many Cold War films we might have chosen for its memorable leadership lessons. The 40-year standoff between the U.S. and the Soviet Union may not have resulted in direct military conflict, but it did spawn a number of terrific films as dramatically appealing as they are informative about leadership.

One of the earliest and best was Stanley Kubrick's *Dr. Strangelove or: How I Learned to Stop Worrying and Love the Bomb*. This 1963 black comedy tells the story of the brilliantly named Jack Ripper, a U.S. Air Force general who goes crazy and orders his bombers to destroy the U.S.S.R. Unlike Ramius, who has a hunch about how to save the world, this madman leader is hell-bent on destroying it. A year later came *Seven Days in May* (1964), a more serious political thriller so well-crafted that it remains a standard of the genre. The film, based on a book written by two Washington insiders, portrays a popular chairman of the Joint Chiefs of Staff who plans to execute a coup d'etat if the president cuts a disarmament deal with the Russians. That same year brought *Fail Safe* (1964), a hauntingly clairvoyant film that warns against the dangers of humans yielding accountability to machines. A technical snafu in a Pentagon computer transmits an incorrect message to a B-52 squadron, and the bombers are ordered to destroy Moscow. Predictably, all hell breaks loose as American and Russian leaders forge an audacious, if extremely costly solution.

Yet when it comes to profoundly important lessons about leadership, none of these films can compete with *The Hunt for Red October*, the tale of a Soviet nuclear submarine captain who defects to the United States. The film is based on the novel of the same name, written by bestselling author Tom Clancy.

Understandably, people wondered where Clancy got so much seemingly top-secret information about the world's nuclear submarine fleets. Simple. Like Jack Ryan, one of the protagonists in *The Hunt for Red October*, he did his homework. And he tapped the public domain. Books like *The World's Missile Systems*, *Combat Fleets of the World*, *The Naval Institute Guide to the Soviet Navy*, and *Janes Fighting Ships* enabled Clancy to describe convincingly all manner of hardware and gizmos, from the electronic details of a Seahawk helicopter's sonar transducer to the operating characteristics of the radar-deceiving Stealth fighter.

Like you or your kids, he even bought an elaborate computer game called "Harpoon" to learn submarine strategy and tactics. All this low-level research paid off in some very high-level results: a string of bestselling books, a win-the-lottery fortune, and pressure from local Republicans to run for Congress.

## A Deadly Serious Search for Freedom

But the hunt in *The Hunt for Red October* is not a game. It is the story of Marko Ramius's search for freedom, and it is art imitating life. In 1975, the executive officer of the Russian destroyer *Storozhevoi* and several coconspirators incarcerated its commanding officer, then shackled the other officers on board and headed for political asylum. Their plan? To cross from Riga, the capital of Latvia, to Sweden, where they would demand reforms in the Soviet system. Approaching its destination, the ship was stopped by aircraft fire. Soon after, the leader of the defection was executed by firing squad. In the film, Captain Ramius (played by Sean Connery) lives. And—as we've pointed out—he succeeds completely, but only after Moscow dispatches fifty-eight attack submarines to hunt him down. They have been ordered to destroy *Red October*, whose superquiet silent propulsion system makes it the first submarine to be invisible to U.S. warning nets in the Atlantic. This gives *Red October*, which carries fifty-six ss-31 short-range attack missiles, first-strike capability. Understandably, the Russians don't want their high-tech submarine's secrets to fall into Western hands, and the Americans don't want a nuclear strike.

But they *do* want *Red October*.

This dilemma fuels a marvelous debate in a Washington, D.C., briefing room. Is Ramius a rogue madman, bent on starting World War III? Should he be immediately hunted down and destroyed? Does anybody have a clue? Enter Jack Ryan (Alec Baldwin), a brilliant CIA analyst with no pretensions to power and a rather casual approach to the conventional wisdom of admirals, generals, and Washington bureaucrats. Put simply, Ryan is the perfect person to come up with a thoroughly unconventional solution. He thinks Ramius is going to defect, not attack.

His reason? He follows a hunch. He acts on an audacious intuitive leap, an almost unconscious use of his experience and knowledge.

Jack Ryan, it turns out, is an intuitive and deeply analytical thinker. He is able to envision a large array of possible solutions to problems (intuiting) and then critically evaluate those alternatives (thinking).

Here's where Ryan's knowledge, skills, and considerable homework fuel his intuition. He believes that Ramius, still mourning the death of his wife one year earlier, not only wants his freedom but also wants to rid the Soviets of their newest first-strike offensive weapon. Not surprisingly, the Washington mandarins initially scoff at Ryan's intuitive hunch. But he finally gets a hearing when Jeffrey Pelt (Richard Jordan), the president's national security adviser and one of the film's little-noticed heroes, asks him to stay after a particularly rough emergency briefing. Listen:

PELT   Let's assume for a minute that you're right and this Russian intends to defect. What do you suggest we do about it?

RYAN   We definitely grab the boat, sir.

PELT   Wait a minute—we're not talking about some stray pilot with a MIG. We're talking about several billion dollars of Soviet state property—they'll want it back.

RYAN   Maybe it's enough then just to get some people on board and inspect it. Call it whatever you want to, a Coast Guard safety inspection.

PELT   So how do we proceed?

RYAN    Well, first, we need to contact the commanders in
        the Atlantic directly. The Russians get one whiff of
        this through the regular communications circuits
        and the game is up. Second, we need to figure out,
        what can we do to help them? We need to devise a
        plan to intercede, ready to go at a moment's notice.
        And third, somebody's got to go out there and
        make contact with Ramius and find out what his
        intentions really *are*.

PELT    Ok. When do you leave?

RYAN    Wait a minute—the general was right, I am not
        field personnel. I am only an analyst . . .

PELT    You're perfect! I can't ask any of these characters
        to go. One, they don't believe in it. Two, they'd
        never stake their reputation on a hunch. Whereas
        you . . .

RYAN    [wryly] . . . are expendable.

PELT    Something like that. I'll give you three days to
        prove your theory correct. After that, I have to hunt
        down Ramius and destroy him. Will you do it?

Of course he will.

Jack Ryan, like Marko Ramius, is a gambler, willing to risk
everything on a hunch. That is what singles him out as a consummate leader. Relying on instinct as well as intellect, he
exemplifies what author Roy Rowan calls *the intuitive manager*

(in his book of the same name), a person whose actions are informed not just by fact, but by feeling as well. Intuition, that rare human capacity to blend together left-brained linear reasoning based on empirical data with wildly circular, creative, and risk-laden right-brained thought, seems, in fact, to define not only Ryan and Ramius, but also a number of the key players in *The Hunt for Red October*.

The tale depends on something we call *intuitive webs*.

## When a Hunch Can Change Everything

Intuition is sadly lacking in most organizations, both military and civilian. No wonder: we seem to value the logical thinking process over the spontaneous "a-ha," the unexpected, wholly serendipitous revelation. We have, in other words, an organizational preference for the coolly rational, for systematic thinkers—people who believe in a rational, mechanistic view of reality. For them, causality and mathematical laws can explain almost everything.

These highly systematic types tend to plan carefully, discard alternatives quickly, conduct ordered searches for more information, and slavishly complete all the steps of any analysis they have begun. For them, making a decision is a purely logical, data-driven process, a left-brained linear play.

Their more intuitive brethren, however, are quite different, preferring instead what seems to be a much more chaotic and circular decision-making process. Think of it as a right-brained savvy that draws on relationships, patterns, and analogies that are often more persuasive and revealing than mere data. They like to read between the lines, trusting their instinctive sense of what's happening around them. They redefine the problem frequently and consider an amazing array of alternatives simultaneously, exploring and abandoning each in a kind of continuous—and seemingly disordered—guessing process.

But lest you think Ryan's intuition is the province only of impulsive, shoot-from-the-hip hotheads, consider its impressive lineage. The ancient Greeks saw intuition as a way to comprehend universal principles. Following one's instincts was, they thought, superior to using sensate calculations. Later great philosophers—most notably Immanuel Kant, the eighteenth-century German philosopher—regarded having a hunch as a kind of inner knowing process by which we acquire knowledge. He made no apologies for his preference for it, arguing that an idea that is supplied by intuition is much more valuable than the kind of knowledge derived merely from the senses or from "scientific" knowledge produced by reasoning or experience. To explore these ideas, suppose we rewrite Ramius's and Ryan's parts in *The Hunt for Red October*. In our imaginary film script, the two have been given ordinary jobs. They are management consultants, high-powered suits, dispensing astonishingly expensive cures for what ails corporations throughout the world.

We catch up with them in an elegant boardroom on the sixtieth floor of a Tokyo skyscraper, where they sit across a shiny table from a group of Japanese executives. The two know nothing about the company; this is their first meeting with its senior executives. Yet the chair of the board asks their opinion about where a multimillion-dollar manufacturing facility should be located. Marko Ramius answers without hesitation, describing the advantages and disadvantages of several sites before finally making his recommendation.

One of the executives listens carefully and then asks: "Whom should we pick for our European marketing director?" Jack Ryan, even though he knows none of the company's executives, quickly describes the right person.

"What about that new alliance we are planning with an American distributor?" wonders another of the Japanese executives. Ryan answers in detail.

What's going on here?

This is no film script. What may look like corporate-style psychic channeling actually happens. In this case, only the names have been changed to protect the consultants, expert intuitives who routinely deliver such irrational revelations to hundreds of clients all over the world for about $1,200 a day. They are hardcore scientists and executives who've labored in startups and studied at places like MIT and the Stanford Research Institute, engineers and physicists who've abandoned the straight life to preach intuitionism, the belief that the best ideas often do not come from purely rational thinking.

For them, Ryan's hunch and Ramius's premonition seem as natural as, well, the paranormal—a kind of enhanced horse sense.

Let's face it: this is weird stuff. Yet it seems that gut feel, paranormal insight—call it what you will—may be part of the

leader's job. The ability to get ideas not just from rational thinking but also from an intuitive flash will continue to produce
profits for consultants.

## Intuition in the Real World

Quinn Spitzer and Ron Evans, who are fascinated by the power
of the hunch, recently reported on a series of executive interviews they did on the subject.[1] Here's what some of the executives they interviewed had to say about the importance of
intuition.

- Scott Davidson, chief executive officer of ICI Acrylics:
  "Gut feel tells you when you have enough information
  to make the right decision."
- Ralph Larsen, chairman and chief executive officer of
  Johnson & Johnson: "Every time I have been burned in
  decision making, it is because I have gone against my
  instincts."
- Richard Teerlink, president and chief executive officer
  of Harley-Davidson: "You may sometimes choose an
  alternative that is not the rational alternative, based on
  gut feel."
- C. K. Prahalad, Harvey C. Fruehauf Professor of Business Administration at the University of Michigan: "One
  of the biggest impediments to effective decision making
  today is that all the literature and all the consultants have
  recommended that emotion and passion be taken out of

management. They think that strategy is a purely analytical exercise."

These personal anecdotes are only the tip of the intuitive iceberg. Executives at Fortune 500 companies like Tenneco and New Jersey Bell have been receiving training in the art of the hunch since the 1980s. Perhaps more convincing is the fact that intuition clubs have been sprouting up at companies like 3M and DuPont. All this has led the influential *Wall Street Journal* to announce that "intuition is *in.*"[2]

It is also the subject of increasing scientific study. A group of neuroscientists at the University of Iowa's College of Medicine, for example, recently wondered about the role intuition plays in the important leadership function of decision making.[3] Their bottom line? Our emotions can actually be helpful in making sound decisions. According to the researchers, a part of the brain located just above the eyes—the ventromedial sector of the prefrontal cortex—serves as a kind of emotional memory bank for huge amounts of data about life's rewards and punishments. When a choice has to be made, we unconsciously mine this databank for hunches and gut feelings that shape and form our behavior. The resulting decision is almost always better than a wholly rational one.

As a result, having a hunch has become respectable. As one enthusiast puts it, "If logical reasoning and scientific analysis have brought knowledge to the crown of human intelligence, then intuition—and its inseparable twin, creativity—form the jewel in the crown."[4]

## Weaving Intuitive Webs

This newly gained regard for hunches makes sense, for they are the elemental threads of *intuitive webs*. Intuitive webs connect two or more people together in a powerful way that goes beyond the rational. Recall how Jack Ryan's solitary gutsy hunch about Marko Ramius's motives and intentions sets in motion a complex sequence of activities in *The Hunt for Red October.*

Such is the influential power of intuition. It's Steven Jobs, in his first incarnation in the 1970s as chief visionary at Apple Computer, "knowing"—when no one else seemed to—that something quite new and quite unproven called *graphic user interface* would forever change the information technology world. Jobs's hunch was, of course, correct. Within months of his intuitive epiphany, easy-to-understand pictures and icons replaced unwieldy DOS commands on computer screens, making computers as easy to use as toasters.

Unlike Jobs, senior managers at Xerox—where the graphic user interface was created—just didn't get it. Almost entirely bereft of intuition, not a single Xerox executive acted on a hunch about the future of personal computers. As a result, caught up in their rational side and unable to tap into their intuitive side, they literally gave away the billion-dollar personal computer market to Microsoft, IBM, and Apple. In computing, Xerox had become a zero, a bunch of "printer-heads," as Jobs derisively called them.

To avoid such a fate, each of us—like Jobs, Ramius, and Ryan—must watch carefully for a turning point illuminated by the light of a strongly believed hunch. Transformed into a single great idea, this gut feeling can settle us on a particular course that changes everything, a road each individual cannot leave but must travel on.

Weaving these solitary ideas into a coherent fabric can create an extraordinary level of organizational effectiveness. Think of individuals or groups who are united by a purpose without a formal institutional presence. Think of the team as a group of connected individuals loosely aligned in a virtual organization rather than a freestanding hierarchy. Forget about power residing only at the apex of the pyramid, or even at the center of a circle. Think of it, instead, as a movable feast, migrating from the center to the perimeter, where—on occasion—the most unlikely employee, or customer, becomes your most valuable creator of a great new idea. Conceive of, as one futurist has put it, "organizations that address the individual and the organization simultaneously, something like the relationship of the bee to the hive."[5]

What's needed, of course, is balance. Spitzer and Evans, whose groundbreaking research yielded the anecdotal evidence we cited on page 14, call this balance "Socrates with a baton."[6]

Translation? Leaders need both analysis *and* intuition. (We would add that the first usually fuels the second. The intuitive "a-ha" almost always is preceded by the exhaustive hard work of logic and reason.) Spitzer and Evans use a metaphor from *Star Trek* to make their point. Leaders need, they argue, to be both Spockian and Kirkian—a blend of Mr. Spock, the man of reason, and Captain Kirk, who frequently operates on gut instinct. There is, in other words, no inherent conflict between reason and intuition; together they constitute the stuff of effective leadership.

Even more powerful are hunches shared in intuitive webs. How do you do this? With whom do you share your hunches?

You look, and you listen. The challenge, of course, is for you to construct highly intricate webs designed not to intercept the paths of flying insects, but the invaluable hunches of those other intuitives around you. To do this, you must become attentive to the vibrations that oscillate in your web, alerting you to the fact that instead of having a guest to digest, you have something much more nourishing: someone to heed very carefully.

The larger the intuitive team, the better. In *The Hunt for Red October*, for example, when Jeffrey Pelt discerns the glimmer of validity in Ryan's explanation of Captain Ramius's plans, intuitive communication begins between the two of them, propelling the film's action forward. In this moment of truth, the two weave the first tentative strands of what is to become an intuitive web. Soon, others add their hunches to this circuitry. There's Seaman Jones (Courtney B. Vance), a sonarman aboard the USS *Dallas*, whose sensitive hearing is outclassed only by his capacity for making educated guesses. And Bart Mancuso (Scott Glenn), commanding officer of the *Dallas*, creates a linking pin in this intuitive web when he takes Jones's hunch seriously.

> JONES    Captain, you may think I'm crazy, but I'll bet
>          that magma displacement was actually some

## *The Hunt for Red October* Intuitive Web

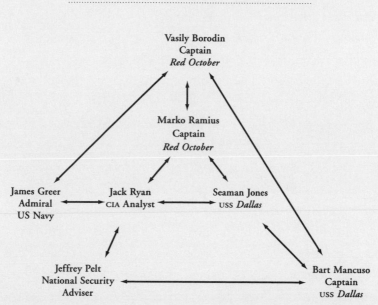

new Russian sub, and it's headed for the Iceland coast.

MANCUSO   Have I got this straight, Jonesy? A 40-million-dollar computer tells you you're chasing an earthquake, but you don't believe it. And you come up with this on your own?

JONES   [uncertain] Yes, sir.

MANCUSO   Relax, Jonesy, you sold me.

Even the Russian ambassador to the United States connects
intuitively with the White House via Pelt when he asks the U.S.
to help find *Red October*.

Before the film is over, we have a loosely woven intuitive
network as complex as a computer chip—guided, as it were,
by an invisible hand, connecting no less than eight people,
some of whom do not even know each other and have never
spoken to each other. Yet, giving credence to the anthem of a
networked age, all are *working together apart*, playing off each
other's hunches.

How do intuitive webs operate in the real world? As is true
in many social systems, reciprocity plays a role. This quid pro
quo enables you to establish a connection between yourself and
other individuals and encourages the flow of rational *and* intuitive judgments. And, just as in Confucian societies, where
close-knit networks known as *guanxi* ensure that all-important
linkage with the "right person," reciprocity ensures intuitive
connections and the webs they make possible.

## Spotting Other Intuitives

The most important task is identifying those who have that
special knack for perceiving truth and fact independent of any
apparent reasoning process. They love to grapple with what
wags call *unstructured problems*. Intuitives are happiest when
dealing with what most of us consider a managerial bad dream:
situations with high levels of uncertainty, little precedent for
action, few facts, fewer predictable variables, and extreme
urgency.

They love a mess.

But how to spot them? No need to trek off to Machu Picchu or to retain a Vedic astrologer. Instead, simply look for people who have what Roy Rowan calls the *eureka factor*. Intuitives, while not disdaining deductive reasoning, structures, committees, and flow charts, prefer to rely on gut instinct and emotion.

They can be recognized instantly by their tendency to exclaim out of the blue, "I've got it!" (In *The Hunt for Red October*, Ryan's exclamation is edgier: "You son of a bitch! . . . Ramius might be trying to defect.") Finally, unlike mere mortals, nothing motivates them like the words "That won't work!"

A *Psychology Today* study of people who possess a high capacity for intuitive insight provides a field guide for recognizing them.[7] Look for colleagues who:

1. **Are quick studies**. They have the ability to see something very briefly—perhaps without even being aware that they are seeing it—and still be able to describe it. Experts call this *perceptual closure on insufficient time* or the *skill of subliminal effect*.
2. **Can see through the murk**. High intuitives are able to fill in the blanks and to know what they are looking at without having all the information. They can separate the wheat from the chaff.
3. **Can find Waldo**. Remember the popular game "Where's Waldo?" conceived by the British illustrator Martin Handford? This game did not just depend on the power of observation. The trick was to find the small but not

completely concealed Waldo as he made his way through crowded airports and railroad stations. Succeeding at this kind of game suggests an intuitive capacity that can be invaluable at work.

4. **Can see the forest for the trees.** This is synthesis, or *gestalt* insight, the ability to put various items together in the mind's eye to construct a whole.

5. **Understand that timing is everything.** People who are intuitive are also acutely sensitive to time. They can cook a 3-minute egg without watching the clock. They seem to know when to buy a stock and when to sell it. On the battlefield, they know when to attack and when to run. This skill is intrinsic to survival and success.

6. **Possess terrific memory.** Remember that childhood game in which someone put a mixture of unrelated items on a table and then, after removing them, asked you to list them all? High intuitives do well at this. They can take in a whole complex scene and remember specific details of it.

7. **Have foresight.** Intuitives seem to know better than mere mortals what's going to happen next. When is the horse going to fall down? When is the skater going to leap off the ice? When is the submarine going to hit the rock?

Making an intuitive web work requires the same funda-mental attention as that paid to any high-performing team. First, there's the all-important need for a clear focus on the task at hand, some overarching goal that each player believes in. In *The Hunt for Red October*, the objective is to prevent war and to acquire some very important military technology. In *your* very real world, this might translate into blocking a competitor's move into a product or service niche that you hope to dominate, or—perhaps more likely—fending off a hostile takeover attempt.

Then there's the marvelous efficacy of deadlines. Nothing captures the attention of the troops like the prospect of missiles raining down over their heads at midnight. Tight deadlines and stretch goals are the glue that holds intuitive webs together.

Delegation, too, drives intuitive thinking. No great hunch has ever been fueled by micromanaging subordinates. In *The Hunt for Red October*, fate turns on a lowly sonarman's ability to do what no one else can—"hear" a silent submarine. And when Bart Mancuso, his commanding officer, utters the words, "Hang on, Jonesy. If I can get you close enough, can you track this sucker?" the young sailor knows that he is truly in the loop, vital to the outcome. He is part of the web, and for the moment he is in charge.

Good characters and good leaders are frequently defined by their ability to make educated guesses. Absolute knowledge may be the stuff of astrophysics, accounting, and calculus—worlds in which accurate, measurable, and reliable information exists. But leaders are not calculating machines. For them, such certainty rarely exists.

Leadership is about hunches, risk, and uncertainty. And that is why intuition—and intuitive webs—are so important. The next time someone walks into your office and announces, "I've got an idea," listen. That crazy hunch just might save the company.

*Jim Lovell (Tom Hanks), Fred Haise (Bill Paxton), and Jack Swigert (Kevin Bacon) fit a square peg into a round hole in Apollo 13, improvising their way out of disaster.*

# TWO

# THE IMPORTANCE OF IMPROVISATION

### *Apollo 13*

## CAST OF CHARACTERS

Jim Lovell  *(Tom Hanks)*

Jack Swigert  *(Kevin Bacon)*

Fred Haise  *(Bill Paxton)*

Ken Mattingly  *(Gary Sinise)*

Gene Kranz  *(Ed Harris)*

Director: Ron Howard

Screenwriters: William Broyles, Jr., and Al Reinert

If you are old enough to remember July 20, 1969—the day the United States led the world to the moon—you probably know exactly where you were when Neil Armstrong stepped down from *Apollo 11*, walked in the Sea of Tranquillity, and kicked up the dust of discovery. Suddenly the moon wasn't just a romantic idea anymore. It had become an attainable reality.

But by April of 1970, the time of the launch of *Apollo 13*, the space program was a yawn for most Americans, who'd been there, done that. Routine procedure. Flight commander Jim Lovell and astronauts Fred Haise and Jack Swigert didn't have much of an audience.

That is, of course, until everything went wrong.

The movie *Apollo 13* (1995) is about leaders and teams brilliantly improvising their way through an unprecedented crisis. The routine "stirring" of oxygen tanks on the spacecraft (what the NASA folks call *housekeeping procedure*), creates a mysterious explosion that cripples the *Odyssey* (*Apollo*'s command module), sending it into a catastrophic countdown toward 100 percent failure. No moon landing, no spaceship, no astronauts.

What's a more intriguing story than that of a high-performance team trained in difficult procedures, carrying out a great project, hell-bent on discovering brave new worlds? And let's add to that, at the dawn of a new age?

Well, probably the story of that same great project going wrong.

The stakes are high, the pace is exhilarating, and the demands on human creativity and will are enormous—and the bigger the project, the bigger the rush of adrenaline and desire to see a potential failure become an inspired success. It's both a leadership nightmare and a leadership adventure in that unexpected but inevitable event that wakes you up to a wonderful, uncomfortable truth about leadership: you can't just rely on training, procedures, guidelines, and manuals to get you through. To transcend mere management—the plodding if expert execution of tasks, goals, and agendas, and the skill to play by some difficult rules—you're going to need to know right off the bat that you can count on nothing.

## Working the Problem

If you love the idea of *that*, of using talent and skill and flying blind, you're probably cut out for leading others through the maze of missions large or small. This demands ingenuity, clever improvisation, flexibility, and the imagination to "work the problem, people!" as flight operations commander Gene Kranz (Ed Harris) puts it in Ron Howard's film of a flight gone wrong.

*Work the problem.*

But what *is* the problem?

You've got reports, records, profiles, predictions, troubleshooters, expert staff, terrific training, assessors, mediators, consultants, and a pile of books. But chances are, you already suspect that the problem will be the one nobody expected.

Start by knowing that. What's sure is that it's all unsure.

Movie audiences love nothing better than watching folks who thought they were signed on for a by-the-book operation having to wing it to survive. The tenacity that's required in such scenarios fuels great films. The cinematic paradigm of the narrow escape is, of course, the sinking ship. And it's riveting stuff,

probably because sinking ships (or disabled spaceships) can
so easily become a metaphor for ambition, knowledge,
hope, and skill. *Titanic*, James Cameron's 1998 blockbuster
movie, didn't rake in the dollars because people die. It raked
them in because heroine Rose—the feisty symbol of human
buoyancy—doesn't.

This familiar story is also played out in the lesser-known
*The Red Tent* (1971), a film starring the late Peter Finch as shaky
leader General Nobile, whose dirigible crashes in the Arctic,
and Sean Connery as his rescuer, Roald Amundsen.

The ability to think well, with optimism, keen judgment,
and creativity, as your ship flounders always determines the outcome of a mission gone wrong. And, as all three films (*Titanic*,
*The Red Tent*, and *Apollo 13*) point out, the goals and procedures
you depend on may have to be transformed into new goals
and new procedures in the blink of an eye. Rescue isn't always
an option, crisis or not. You're on your own, supplies are
limited, and you will, hell or high water, succeed.

*Apollo 13* tells the story of a moment along the timeline to
the millennium that we are wise to remember, when the right
stuff was very nearly not enough, when one of mankind's
greatest engineering feats was transformed in seconds into space
junk hurtling out of control.

## Murphy's Law in Action

*Apollo 13* unabashedly celebrates all the gee-whiz gizmos and
gadgets of high tech. All the *cryos*, AC *bus undervolts*, *reactant
valves*, CSMs, MOCRs, and TELMUS make your eyes roll back as

the astronauts' instrumentation problem becomes your comprehension problem. At the same time, the film explains why airplanes fall out of the sky and nuclear power plants melt down. That whatever-can-go-wrong-will-go-wrong pragmatism is revealed in a scene vaguely reminiscent of the film *Fantastic Voyage* (1966), in which a submarine full of doctors is shrunken to microscopic size and injected into an injured man's bloodstream.

Here the camera similarly whisks you through *Apollo 13*'s electric bays, whirring motors, pumps, and oxygen tanks, down wires and across circuits, along pipes and fans and valves; and you "become" the snafu that almost did in astronauts Jim Lovell, Fred Haise, and Jack Swigert.

Jim Lovell's eerily calm radio transmission, "Houston, we have a problem," was, it turns out, the last link in a chain of events that seems mundane, the kind of fuse-blowing, circuit-breaking annoyance that propels you to your basement, flashlight in hand. But *Odyssey* was dying, its death throes sounding like the awful metallic moans that preceded the *Titanic*'s plunge.

The story behind this historic spaceship malfunction might have happened in any manufacturing plant where communications are, let's say, incomplete. Several years before the flight, the voltage levels in all the *Apollo* spaceships had been changed, yet one of the subcontractors responsible for providing thermostats was never informed. When, during the ill-starred flight, one of the astronauts turned on the fans inside the oxygen tank, the resulting electrical arc caused the explosion that would cripple *Apollo 13*.

But there are no such screw-ups in creating the film *Apollo 13*. Sure, the NASA logo worn on the astronauts' flight suits is wrong, and the Mr. Coffee–type drip pots so much in evidence in Houston weren't in use at the time, and you can see cars parked on the launch pad at liftoff. But these trivialities do little to disrupt the movie's docudrama authenticity. Like other films directed by Ron Howard, *Apollo 13* uses a large arsenal of cinematic tricks. The music—you expect "Ode to the Common Man" at any moment—swells as the astronauts bond, brothers on a dangerous quest. The special effects are unnervingly real, combining *Jurassic Park*–quality visuals with sound that shakes the theater as the 363-foot long *Saturn V* rocket lifts off. The various dockings, maneuvers, and undockings and the astronauts floating in zero gravity—made possible by hundreds of hours of shooting in the "Vomit Comet," a modified Boeing 707 flying a sickeningly parabolic roller-coaster ride—have all the choreographic beauty set so nicely to Strauss in Stanley Kubrick's definitive *2001: A Space Odyssey* (1968).

But more than anything else, *Apollo 13* draws its strength and authenticity from the fierce loyalty Howard and the screenwriters paid to Jim Lovell's book *Lost Moon*, from which it was adapted. The author was ebullient about his text. "Listen," he is reported to have told Howard, "just tell our story as it happened, and you'll have a thrilling movie."

He was right, because the cosmic-sized question *Apollo 13* keeps on asking for 2 hours and 20 minutes, one that hooks you from launch to splashdown even though you know precisely how the story ends, is this: how do three men, sardined and freezing for 87 hours in a tumbling and pitching spacecraft the size of a small automobile with no electricity and only a couple of hours of oxygen left, manage to survive and execute a pinpoint return to earth, landing only hundreds of yards from the recovery ship? *Time* magazine's film critic Richard Corliss put these complications this way: "Imagine a minivan towing a small boat to the beach. The minivan is *Odyssey*, *Apollo 13*'s command module . . . the boat is *Aquarius*, the lunar module. Now imagine that, on a nowhere stretch of road, your van just about blows up. How do you get home?"[1]

Don't think the NASA folks weren't prepared for just about anything to go wrong. These people are at the very top of their game in knowledge and skill. They have that ideal combination of talents that defy commonplace doubts. They troubleshoot the most complex and unexpected problems every step of the way. True, NASA had never anticipated an accident like *Apollo 13*'s, but they'd learned this remarkable fact, as described by Gene Kranz: "The training was such that by the time you finished the process, you had the confidence that, given a few minutes, you could solve any problem. That's all there was to it. And it didn't matter what the size, what the magnitude, what the origin of the problem was. The fact was that you could solve any problem that came up."[2]

The problem in *Apollo 13* is technology gone awry with time running out. On occasion, though, it's the human factor, as when command module pilot Jack Swigert (Kevin Bacon) loses it during reentry. You can hear the panic in his voice as something goes terribly wrong aboard *Apollo 13*.

SWIGERT   [alarm signal in background] What's the story
          here? I got a corridor light. We're coming in too
          shallow. I'm going to manual.

HAISE     Houston, switching to SES.

SWIGERT   OK, we're at three GS, five GS. We're coming in
          too steep. I'm gonna stay in this roll and see if
          I can pull us out. We're at eight GS. Nine. Ten.
          [continuous dual alarms in background] We're
          at twelve GS.

LOVELL    Twelve GS. We're burning up!

## Simulating Reality

But it never happened! There was no fire on *Apollo 13*, no loss
of control on reentry. Swigert's error actually occurred during
a simulation. And, although they didn't make it to the moon,
all three astronauts—as everyone knows—survived the actual
mission. The reason? They had made their trip hundreds of
times before, without ever leaving Houston. Much of their
training was in simulators, machines designed to mimic space
flight. The idea was to practice correct procedures and ways of
coping with unexpected problems.

Watch how these scenarios are run—good enough isn't
good enough. Perfectionist Ken Mattingly (Gary Sinise) spot-
checks himself, demands replays even when he's performing
perfectly. And the scenarios aren't simple—when Jack Swigert
misses a booby trap in training, one of the engineers mutters,

"Even Mattingly didn't get it the first time." But they're back in the simulator until he gets it right.

You can get the same kind of virtual flight experience at home using your personal computer. And if simulators can be used to teach humans how to land on the moon and enable you to practice landings on your PC, they can also be used to prevent that new marketing plan from crashing and burning.

Welcome to the world of space-age simulations for leaders and managers. One of the best, created by the Center for Creative Leadership, is as unashamedly low-tech as *Mercury*, the first space capsule. But it made a pioneering step toward bringing the science of simulation to business and management.

Going by the code name "Looking Glass" (because teams of participants run virtual competing glass manufacturing companies while consultants and psychologists observe and debrief them), it helps participants learn about themselves and their leadership behaviors. The center claims that Looking Glass teaches participants how to "steer clear of problems, plot strategic possibilities, and juggle tactical concerns; make tough decisions, while fending off a multitude of issues and plowing through an overload of information." This simulation might be as useful to astronauts as it is to more earthbound leaders.

But those PCs we mentioned have changed everything, creating a whole new market for these simplified representations of reality that can cost hundreds of thousands of dollars when custom built.

It's worth it. Well-constructed models enable managers to "run a scenario" to see how a plan of action might work in a risk-free, fail-safe environment before launching it into the real world, just as a pilot might spend hundreds of hours in a flight simulator before taking the controls of a commercial jet.

What better way for managers to learn how to compete effectively in the whitewater world of global business without sinking in the rapids? Bell Canada, for example, uses a computer game called "TeleSim" to teach its managers how to keep from crashing in the chaotic new deregulated telecommunications world. In the simulation, players create marketing strategies (complete with segmentation, product positioning, and product portfolio design) in order to compete with Bell Canada's competitors. General Electric uses a similar action-learning simulation to show managers at its newly acquired Tungsram lighting division in Hungary how to build a business in a developing market economy. Another simulation comes packed with a dark sense of humor, showing on its opening screen a ship cruising in a perfectly calm sea. By the end of the game, if a team is performing poorly, the ship sinks.

All this, of course, goes beyond mere technical skill and spreadsheet savvy. The real point of these simulations is to get at the human factor. Just as an astronaut's performance in the *Apollo* simulator could affect his future in the space program, so too can your performance in a business simulation become an important assessment of your talent to lead. After all, under the lightning-quick speed and data overload of virtual business games, each participant's capacity for leadership and teamwork becomes apparent.

Some people derisively call computer simulations "games," citing their inability to duplicate conditions and forces operating in the real business world. And virtual reality can get pretty wacky. One simulation firm was asked to develop a simulation that would train employees about infrequently used plant-operating policies. The company's solution? A simulation starring dueling robots.

But aboard *Apollo 13*, it was deadly serious. This out-of-the-box idea to use the lunar landing module as a lifeboat wasn't dreamt up on the spur of the moment by Jim Lovell (Tom Hanks). When he asks Fred Haise (Bill Paxton), "How long does it take to power up the LEM?" he was enacting a procedure conceived years earlier and practiced—in simulation—only weeks before the launch, a drill that everyone thought would never have to be used.

## A Bit of Common Sense

It's not just technology that brings the astronauts back to earth. Common sense, that most widely distributed yet rarely used quality, looms large in every scene in *Apollo 13*, driving solutions to seemingly unsolvable problems. Levelheaded sensibility is palpable as team members search their personal memory banks for feasible alternatives each time they face a new problem, using helpful metaphors. *Suppose you need to abandon ship. What you need, very quickly, is a lifeboat. That's a strong buoyant craft used in an emergency, especially in saving lives at sea. No problem that we're in deep space. Conclusion? The lunar module can be our lifeboat!*

Such common sense has recently been applied at Ford Motor Company, where its Business Leadership Initiative gets teams of employees to take on 100-day projects aimed at reducing costs and increasing profits. One group recently emerged from this experience concluding that a pile of money could be saved if the expensive Kevlar gloves used by the company's sheet metal workers could be washed and reused rather than thrown away. Another found that if traveling engineering teams used mobile phones rather than hotel phones, rented apartments rather than using hotels, and drove company pool cars rather than rentals, they could save thousands. Another team learned how to apply some very down-to-earth principles from a senior executive who told how he succeeded with a boyhood fish business. Like something out of *Aesop's Fables*, it contained a lot of wisdom. You:

1. borrow some money in the morning, which you
2. use to buy fish and ice and rent a stall in the town market; then you
3. price below the competition so that you can
4. sell one batch of fish, then use the proceeds to buy and sell another batch in order to
5. repay the loan at the end of the day and
6. make a profit.

His point? Shorter inventory cycles and higher return on capital are both possible and beneficial. "Business is really very simple," rhapsodized the Ford executive to a reporter. He's right, of course. All it takes is a little common sense. But doing the impossible also requires support from others, like those engineers staring pleadingly into their consoles back at Mission Control, trying to translate strings of data into a solution. Their greatest fear is silence. Even five seconds of stillness could mean the worst: that the "down link," that communications umbilical cord joining Houston to *Odyssey*, had been severed. But the crackling static is replaced every time with the almost too calm voices of the astronauts. Their crisp "Roger that" and "Understand, Houstons" sound like the reassuring cabin announcements made by the pilot of a commercial jet that's just lost an engine. The same kind of just-sit-back-and-relax-everything's-going-to-be-fine tone is hurtled back from Houston. "Thirteen, we still have that venting pushing you around. How're you doing?"; "*Aquarius*, we've got some burn data for you fellas"; and "Jim, we're working on a procedure down here for you" suggest unmistakably that the guys in the air are getting expert advice from the guys on the ground.

This is the epitome of what has come to be called a high-performance team. And flight operations commander Gene Kranz comes off as a leader's leader and a master teambuilder. After that first surge of crisis, Kranz calms the room by giving quick, deft advice on immediate tasks, as well as on behavior, and moves with calm assurance from console to console, gathering information and evaluations from his guys. He guides hundreds of people into cooperative problem solving.

His approach? First, he is a "good news" leader. His approach to catastrophe is a lesson in applied optimism: find something, anything, that is positive, and then keep the optimism going strong. He fuels this positive mental attitude by focusing on the big picture ("Failure is not an option!") while at the same time worrying about his own reputation ("NASA has never lost an astronaut in space, and we're sure as hell not going to lose one on my watch!"). It works. When Kranz's boss whines, "This could be the worst disaster NASA ever experienced," Kranz can't help but reply, "With all due respect, sir, I believe this is gonna be our finest hour."

Second, Kranz hears perfectly the pitch of knowledge and assurance and selects from dozens of skilled opinions the one that's best. Sure, everyone's determined to solve the problem, but everyone's got a different idea of how to do it. Kranz is able to choose among a cacophony of conflicting opinions.

Obviously, getting the astronauts back to earth, solving the seemingly unsolvable, will depend less on two high-profile leaders than it does on two groups of people acting in unity—in space and on earth—doing the impossible by simply plugging away, pushing urgently for continuous, incremental innovation, and refinement of a stunningly broad array of competing ideas. In *Apollo 13*, as in organizations, it's teams, not leaders, that spell the difference between success and failure. They've checked their egos at the door; they're willing to listen to each other. Think of it as collective leadership.

*Apollo*-like teams have made all the difference lately in some very down-to-earth organizations, cutting production cycles, reducing the costs of developing new products, and shortening delivery time. At General Electric's circuit breaker business, high-performance teams have cut order backlogs from two months to two days and slashed delivery time from three weeks to three days. Owens-Corning has increased productivity by 60 percent. At Xerox, customer service ratings skyrocketed by 80 percent while inventory costs have been reduced by $200 million per year. As they did in *Apollo 13*, extraordinary achievements like these depend on the key processes found in all high-performing teams: problem analysis, spirited debate, choosing alternatives, and brainstorming to generate new and better ideas.

## Stretch Goals

But what fuels such human magic? The challenge of *stretch goals*, those immense milestones and athletic leaps that only happen when you're doing things you didn't think possible. They're audacious, they're challenging, and they're simply put. *Crush Adidas* (Nike, 1960s). *Become the Harvard of the West* (Stanford University, 1940s). *Become a $125 Billion Company by the Year 2000* (Wal-Mart, 1990). And one of history's boldest stretch targets: *I believe this nation should commit itself to achieving the goal, before this decade is out, of landing a man on the moon and returning him safely to the Earth* (John F. Kennedy, NASA speech, May 25, 1961).

The route to achieving stretch goals can be circuitous indeed. After all, when situations change, you've got to change with them, using all the brainpower and tools on hand. Is it easy? The truth is, even high-performance pros resist the unexpected changes of procedure that occur. Shifting tracks is always unnerving. New personnel change chemistry, the studied moves that team members establish as a kind of psychic choreography—you've probably felt it, that perfect sync with your colleagues that keeps the ball rolling smoothly. And it's a hard thing to let go of, especially when the stakes are high. In *Apollo 13*, the scheduled crew can't make the flight, so the guys slated for *Apollo 14* are brought in to do the job. Are they ready? Of course they are. But when surefire team member Mattingly, the rock of the mission, is bumped off the team and replaced by party guy Jack Swigert, a lot of glances are exchanged. The unspoken message is clear, all eyes saying *no way*.

The big question—and every skilled rookie who has replaced a master has felt it circulating in the resistant air around him or her—is, "Can the new kid do what he was not slated to do?" Could Swigert hack it? After all, time was short and he wasn't *supposed* to be there!

But *Apollo 13* reminds us that what's supposed to happen sometimes does not. And that's when leaders explore the *real* unknown.

By improvising.

These people are constantly transforming their materials and procedures into new materials and procedures. The real test is how to push beyond the recognized limits of function and discover new capabilities. This, clearly, is the motivating, saving skill that defines this crisis leadership. This is one of the oldest ideas around—transformation and success require an ability to recognize the unusual capacities of objects and supplies.

*Use what you've got*—imagination—or think of Kranz's leading words, "I don't care what something was designed to do, I care what it *can* do!" Keep track of all the beautiful substitutions that occur in the *Apollo 13* crisis—the lunar module becomes a space lifeboat for the endangered astronauts; the earth becomes an unlikely "fixed point" guidance target during a fuel burn; amps meant to flow from the lunar module to the *Odyssey* are, at Ken Mattingly's brilliant suggestion, reversed to create a lifesaving surge of power to the lunar module; fuel tanks meant for lunar orbit are used as burn systems for a safe

return to the earth's atmosphere; and a weird collage of duct
tape, manual book covers, and plastic bags becomes a vital filter
to solve a carbon dioxide "situation":

ENGINEER      Gene, we have a situation brewing with the
              carbon dioxide. We have a $CO_2$ filter problem
              on the lunar module. Five filters on the LEM,
              which were meant for two guys for a day and
              a half. So I told the doc . . .

FLIGHT        They're already up to eight on the gauges.
SURGEON       Anything over fifteen, you get impaired judg-
              ment, blackouts, the beginnings of brain
              asphyxia.

KRANZ         What about the scrubbers on the command
              module?

ENGINEER      They take square cartridges. The ones on the
              LEM are round.

KRANZ         Tell me this isn't a government operation.

ENGINEER      It just isn't a contingency we've remotely
              looked at. Those $CO_2$ levels are going to be get-
              ting toxic.

KRANZ         Well, I suggest you gentlemen invent a way to
              put a square peg in a round hole, rapidly.

It can't be put more directly. Kranz is asking—no, ordering—his engineers to do the impossible. No discussion. No task
force. No time.

But sometimes this throwing down of the gauntlet, this kind of directness, pays off. Soon, the head engineer has gathered a small team and is dumping assorted odd items onto a table; the items duplicate those available to the astronauts on the LEM.

The conversation that ensues among the engineers tells us all we need to know about why stretch goals and impromptu transformations work. "Ok people, listen up," he says. "The people upstairs handed us this one, and we've gotta come through. We've gotta find a way to make this [holds up square object] fit into the hole for this [holds up round object] using nothing but that [points to the items on the table]. Let's get it organized. Let's build a filter. Better get some coffee going, too." The resulting contraption looks ridiculous as hell, but it saves the astronauts' lives, and the mission.

Simulations. Teamwork. Stretch goals. All orderly and well planned, just like an engineer or an astronaut and (we might add) a manager likes it. But what really saved the *Apollo 13* mission, what turned it into a "successful failure," was improvisation, the same kind of impromptu spontaneity that characterizes the world of theater and music. Giving up the linear and the predictable and the manageable for chaos and perplexity may not seem like a sound management strategy, and it is not. But it is, increasingly, what leadership is all about, bringing with it just what organizations need badly these days: the ability to adapt, the capacity to learn, and the inventiveness to innovate.

The point is that successful leadership sometimes looks more like a night at Second City or a scene from *Alice in Won-*

*derland* than an orderly progression based on careful planning. Consider a classic case: the introduction of Honda motorcycles into the United States in the early 1960s. Honda had planned to gain a wedge in the market by introducing their larger, more powerful motorcycles into a market seemingly transfixed with horsepower and chrome. The plan was set. They'd launch in California and let the wave of demand head east. But then the plan went wrong. West Coast freeways were nothing like the (then) tiny roads of Japan. The motorcycle engines failed when trying to keep up with the relentless 80-mile-per-hour speeds on the interstates. It looked like the best—and best-planned— intentions had gone awry. But, as the story goes, a Honda executive, riding one of the much more diminutive 50-c.c. Supercubs, met a Sears buyer in a supermarket parking lot. The rest, as they say, is history. Honda's smaller bikes became the new "gold standard."

Happenstance changed everything, including how motor- cycles are produced, marketed, and distributed worldwide. As several scholars who study the salutary effects of the unre- hearsed business ad lib put it, "Success flowed from a series of highly unlikely occurrences: the initial shipment of Super- cubs to the U.S., even though conventional wisdom indicated it was a big-bike market; the chance meeting with the Sears buyer; the willingness of Honda's U.S. managers to pursue a serendipitous encounter. Honda's managers did not feel bound by their original plan; they were prepared to work with the sit- uation they faced—in other words, to improvise."[3]

We'd call those inventive Honda managers *leaders*.

## Getting Home

There's no question that by the time *Odyssey* splashes down, nobody's wasting time thinking of what was *supposed* to happen or worrying about the *intended* function of anyone or anything. The *Apollo 13* mission, in which the original goal was aborted, and a new, even more challenging goal was achieved, is a testament to creative thinking, to "winging it." So put aside your disbelief when you have that strange, never-tried-before idea, the one that might just sound a little crazy. Get out your duct tape and go at it, because you never can tell when a little improvisation might save the day. It did for Jim Lovell when he was returning from a World War II mission.

Here's his story about the remarkable power of improvisation, a power that saved his "ship" twice.

LOVELL   My radar had jammed and my homing signal was gone because someone in Japan was using the same frequency; it was leading me away from where I'm supposed to be. And I'm looking down at this big black ocean. So I flip on my map light and suddenly, Zap! Everything shorts out right there in the cockpit, my instruments are gone, my lights are gone, and I can't even tell what my altitude is. I know I'm running out of fuel, and I'm thinking of ditching in the ocean, and I look down there and there in the darkness, there's this green trail. It's like a long carpet that's just laid out beneath me. It was the algae. That phosphorescent stuff that gets churned up in the wake of a big ship. It was just leading me home. If my cockpit lights hadn't shorted out, there's no way I would ever have seen that. You never know what events are going to transpire to get you home.

*Mr. Keating (Robin Williams) challenges tradition in* Dead Poets Society *by getting his students to change their perspectives.*

# THREE

# The Failed Promise of Heroic Leadership

## Dead Poets Society

### Cast of Characters

John Keating *(Robin Williams)*
Neil Perry *(Robert Sean Leonard)*
Todd Anderson *(Ethan Hawke)*
Knox Overstreet *(Josh Charles)*
Charlie Dalton *(Gale Hansen)*

Director: Peter Weir
Screenwriter: Tom Schulman

Films that celebrate teachers and students and the magic they create together have always provided unforgettable lessons for anyone who seeks to lead. Perhaps that is because effective leadership is so inextricably linked to the ability both to instruct and to learn. Surely when you get people to focus their energies on a singular vision and aspiration for the enterprise—to embrace the *big* picture—a transformation occurs. You're no longer CEO, CFO, or CIO, but instead you become what some have begun to call "CLO,"—chief *learning* officer.

This ability to return to the classroom seems to differentiate successful leaders and organizations from the also-rans. It is no wonder: leadership *is* teaching. It's about helping people discover the joy of digesting new ideas, of embracing different business models quickly, and of searching continually for new knowledge. It's about challenging dominant paradigms and existing orthodoxies, and destroying illusions. It's about dialogue, not monologue. It's about *really* communicating your vision and getting others to share your sense of purpose. It's the so-called "learning organization," the brainchild of MIT management guru Peter Senge.

## Leader as Teacher

And take notice. Teaching—and learning—are no longer regarded as the New Age, pie-in-the-sky "soft" stuff of leadership. They are critical to success. Organizations must be able to learn in order to survive. Management scholar Michael Porter puts it this way: "The companies that are going to be able to become successful, or remain successful, will be the ones that can learn fast, can assimilate this learning, and develop new insights; companies are going to have to become much more like universities."[1]

Think back to all the teachers you encountered in your high school or college days, and chances are you'll recall a profound first encounter with a great leader, a teacher who helped you change your life. Or take a look at the people who are teaching your own kids, in the classroom or on a competitive athletic field, inspiring them to experience a passionate interest in learning for the first time. The links between teaching and leading are right in front of you.

Or, you can watch a movie that probes the relationship between leadership and teaching, and be well entertained. Movies about teachers, no matter how far they may stretch the realities of education and instruction (and some stretch them pretty far), almost always hit their audience with a hard emotional punch.

Teachers, even the bad ones, remind us of the human need for a guiding presence, a leader, to awaken us to the best of ourselves and to smack us, like a caring doctor, into the real breathing of our lives. Teachers are often not only our best but our first experience of effective or ineffective leadership. Movies trust us to remember that.

Teacher movies, no matter what the outcome of the plot, rarely fail to teach resonant lessons in leadership. These movies are really about the art of inspiration, transformation, and communication, breaking through boundaries to help others create more productive and successful lives. As a result, teacher movies often have a surefire formulaic approach you may have come to recognize:

1. A group of students are unmoved or overwhelmed by the tasks of life and learning before them.
2. Their teacher is met with resistance and challenge.
3. Finally, with talent, initiative, discipline, and feeling, the teacher makes successful contact with the students in the nick of time—and learns something along the way.

Consider such early films as the genre setter *Goodbye, Mr. Chips* (1939), in which Robert Donat plays a classics teacher who makes conjugating Latin verbs almost fun. This film is as much about the development of a teacher as it is about the education of students. Mr. Chips, after a rocky start, becomes a much-admired teacher.

Reform, however, is the raison d'être in *Blackboard Jungle*, a 1955 film starring Glenn Ford as teacher Richard Dadier, who almost singlehandedly transforms an inner-city school dominated by punks and thugs. Along the way, while trying to educate his students (one of whom is played by Sidney Poitier), Dadier receives an education in teenage criminal behavior. More recently, the career of Jaime Escalante, high school math teacher extraordinaire, was dramatized in *Stand and Deliver* (1987). In a movie that makes the gang of ruffians in *Blackboard Jungle* look like mere mischief makers, these hair-netted hoods are not only undisciplined, disobedient, and rebellious, they're powerful. But Escalante knows that they're schoolboys underneath all that macho. As a teacher, he does for logarithms what Mr. Chips did for Latin declensions. His special talent is the ability to get barrio hoodlums (some of whom keep two sets of textbooks, one at school and one at home, since they don't want to be seen carrying books) to love to learn. His trick is a combination of showbiz and pedagogical strategy, and he succeeds marvelously. His entire class passes the near-impossible National Advanced Placement calculus test, so difficult that only 2 percent of students nationwide pass it. They might as well have won the World Series and the Super Bowl.

Even films in which the teacher fails, like the classic *The Browning Version* (1951), about a fiercely militant Latin teacher hated by everyone he teaches, or the French film *Tous les Matins du Monde (All the Mornings of the World)* (1991), in which a music teacher's student betrays his own blossoming talent to become a shallow, fawning court musician, follow a similar arc. Ultimately, the students are changed by their recognition of their teacher's human failure to lead or by a devastating recognition of their own failure to learn.

But if you ask any moviegoer today to name his or her favorite teacher movies, the answer would almost certainly include *Dead Poets Society* (1989), a film that transports you into the oppressively charming world of a prep school where individuality is repressed and tradition is worshipped. Part of *Dead Poets'* attraction is its sheer beauty.

Picture yourself on the grounds of a very old and very exclusive prep school sometime in the 1950s. It's the beginning of the fall term and the boys—yes, this is a boys' school—are returning to campus. Parents are saying their good-byes. A bagpiper outside of the chapel sanctuary plays *Scotland the Brave*. Inside, four boys carrying banners that read, "Tradition," "Honor," "Discipline," and "Excellence" lower their flags and take their seats. The headmaster, a stern-looking man in full academic regalia, intones "the light of knowledge" as an elderly alumnus lights the candle of one of the students in the choir. A flock of geese rise from a nearby pond.

"The light of knowledge shall be passed from old to young," declares the headmaster.

Welton Academy, nestled in the hills of Vermont, is clearly a place that reveres custom and convention. This unchanging commitment to time-honored practice has been a formula for success. Welton, we soon discover, is one of the best prep schools in the country, regularly sending more than 75 percent of its graduating students on to Ivy League colleges.

## Revolution in the Air

An early scene in *Dead Poets Society* has English teacher John Keating (Robin Williams) mischievously whistling the opening notes of Tchaikovsky's 1812 Overture as he leads his astonished students out of their classroom. Their destination? A trophy case containing old athletic team photographs, which he uses as props as he expounds on the importance of the ancient maxim *Carpe diem!*

Later, back in the classroom, he exhorts his students to *seize the day* by doing the unthinkable, tearing out the introductory chapter of their brand-new poetry textbooks. "Keep ripping, gentlemen," he orders. "This is a battle, a war, and the casualties could be your hearts and souls."

There's revolution in the air. This is no ordinary prep school class. Nor is this a typical prep school teacher. An alumnus of Welton Academy (he calls it "*Hell*ton") and freshly hired, Keating clearly intends to change things. As film critic Desson Howe writes, "He is the English teacher come to shake the Academy down, come to show 'em that somewhere among the three RS is an immensely pleasurable P for poetry."[2] At the very least, he'll get these sheltered kids to spread their wings.

Keating appears to be the genuine agent of change everyone has been waiting for—someone who could be courageous enough and perhaps crazy enough to shake up Welton's hoary tradition and bring the place into the twentieth century, finding an antidote to the culture of stodgy smugness in which Welton comforts itself. With his swagger, his maniacal looks, and his newest-man-on-the-faculty insouciance, John Keating has the charisma and the teaching savvy to get to the hearts and minds of his students. More important, he seems to have fun doing it.

But can he do the same with other, perhaps more critical constituencies like fellow teachers, administrators, and parents? Can he break through the stifling bureaucracy that has for so long governed Welton? Can he, as Archimedes suggested, find a lever long enough to move his world? Keating, in fact, has four levers—students, parents, faculty, and assorted bureaucrats—and he'll need each of them if he is to change Welton Academy.

What makes *Dead Poets Society* so compelling is its depiction of this inspirational and charismatic teacher who succeeds in stirring his students to experience passion, self-revelation, and the thrill of free thinking.

How could he fail? Listen:

KEATING    [referring to the boys in the old photographs in
           the trophy case] They're not that different from
           you, are they? Same haircuts. Full of hormones,
           just like you. Invincible, just like you feel. The
           world is their oyster. They believe they're des-
           tined for great things, just like many of you;
           their eyes are full of hope, just like you. Did
           they wait until it was too late to make from their
           lives even one iota of what they were capable?
           Because, you see, gentlemen, these boys are now
           fertilizing daffodils. But if you listen real close,
           you can hear them whisper their legacy to you.
           Go on, lean in. Listen, you hear it?—Carpe—
           hear it?—Carpe, carpe diem, seize the day, boys,
           make your lives extraordinary.

## What's Missing?

There's a lot of gusto here, a lot of promise. But is change really
in the air?

Maybe not, because at the same time that he inspires, Keating fails in several critical ways. Perhaps that's why what is even
more compelling about *Dead Poets Society* is that its subtleties
allow us to esteem particular *heroic elements* of leadership over
the equally necessary *practical demands* of leadership, reminding
us of a common misconception about what makes a really good
leader.

The sad truth is that if you were to emulate John Keating's leadership principles in *Dead Poets Society*, you might be loved, but you would very probably be fired.

So what's so bad about John Keating? He seems to have so much going for him! He's genuinely charming, and is enthusiastic about his subjects (poetry and literature). He is able to bring humor and fresh perspective to texts and ideas; shows affectionate interest in each of his students; and has noble ambitions to identify individualistic freedom, defy oppressive traditions represented by bullying and pedantic administrators, and encourage his students to get the most out of life by unearthing their own passionate natures. Like Keating's initially skeptical and then adoring students, you'll probably be swept along by the man's sheer charisma and his unconventional approach to teaching.

In his first class, Keating reveals himself as a new kind of leader—authoritative but a bit like a kid himself, able to play with ideas and lessons. This reputation has preceded him— "Mr. Keating was a hell-raiser!" exclaims one student. What's more, Keating knows how to banter easily with his pupils, teasing them about their names and their attitudes, calling to them in mock macho tones, "Huddle up!" as if he is a coach prepping a new team and not a poetry instructor addressing his first class.

He asserts his disinterest in any routine that opposes heartfelt self-expression or the power of personal voice. He also asserts his fearlessness in confronting established curricula he believes is destructive to his students' ability to think for themselves. Keating guides them toward the raw passions of the poets he himself admires—"Thoreau, Whitman, Shelley.

The biggies." (And all of these writers, not coincidentally, are canonized trailblazers—Whitman for his focus on self-assertions and for exploring new poetic forms, Thoreau for his independent retreat from society to embrace the natural world, and Shelley for his poetic rebellions against tyranny and convention.) Keating makes poetry—the project at hand—the necessary center of his students' lives by presenting it with a glamorous, seductive power that eclipses other pursuits. In short, he throws out old ways and creates a new, riveting focus for attention.

Powerful stuff, to say the least. He cries out rallying phrases from the poetry of Walt Whitman (whose most famous work, *Song of Myself*, is an assertion of self, desire, and joyful living), scrawling on the blackboard Whitman's line "I sound my barbaric yawp over the rooftops of the world!" as a sort of mission statement for the boys. He challenges them to accomplish physical tasks as well, as metaphors for spiritual conditions, drawing immediate physical links between felt strength and written expression.

What's going on here?

Like many strong leaders, Keating presents himself as a revolutionary, a man equipped to challenge and rebel against existing order, and able to enlist others to his spirit of defiance and individualism. And the kind of revolutionary spirit that Keating possesses has lately gotten a good name in management and leadership circles, all because of a man named Jack Welch and one of his acolytes, management consultant and guru Noel Tichy. Welch is, of course, the diminutive one-time hockey fanatic who has singlehandedly transformed General

Electric into one of the most emulated corporations in the world. GE's status and Welch's role in its creation are not only commendable, but justifiable: since he became CEO in 1983, the market value of GE has increased more than tenfold. And Tichy is the man who has chronicled his patron's rise to preeminent power among the chieftains of the Fortune 100 in his extravagantly entitled book *Control Your Destiny or Someone Else Will: Lessons in Mastering Change—the Principles Jack Welch Is Using to Revolutionize General Electric.*

## The Revolutionary at GE

What is Tichy's take on Welch? His boss is, at heart, John Keating: a rebel, a firebrand, a rabble-rouser out to do nothing less than bring radical and fundamental change to his company. Part of this revolution has been bloody, as almost everyone knows. Welch's take-no-prisoners style of leadership resulted in the loss of more than 170,000 jobs. And that was only the start. As Tichy reports, "[Welch] has taken the established order at GE and thrown it out the window; he presided over the elimination of scores of the company's businesses and over one-third of its jobs—affecting a group as large as the population of Salt Lake City. As for the employees who remain, Welch has challenged everything they thought they knew."[3] All of this is reduced to a series of checklists in the book's appendix, entitled "Handbook for Revolutionaries."

More important to us, though, is the author's penetrating commentary on the relationship between drama and revolution, which sounds remarkably like what is going on in *Dead*

*Poets Society*. A corporate revolution is a particular kind of drama—a tragedy, perhaps, always with a catharsis and hopefully with a happy ending. For the people involved in the play, it's as gripping and deep as any classical plot. We think of corporations as machines, but they are really more like theatrical troupes: ideas, dialogue, and actions flow among the cast. Managers in the company are part of an ensemble cast demonstrating their skills and magnetism as they perform.

In Keating's classroom, ideas, dialogue, and actions flow freely, but there doesn't seem to be much study of poetry text going on. Instead, Keating guides his students through a series of "life lessons" on the necessity of gaining a unique perspective, on the dangers of conforming to social conventions, on the power of personal vision, and—in an exhausting scene of energetic, aggressive teaching—on how to speak from the heart.

Todd Anderson (Ethan Hawke), the shiest and most resistant of Keating's students—the troubled team player—explodes with an angry, raw, and improvised poem as the direct result of Keating's fearless probing. It's a breakthrough, and the students sit in amazement at the magic they have witnessed.

"Don't you forget this," Keating whispers emphatically as Todd takes deep breaths of triumph and relief. Thanks to Keating, Todd has risen to heights he *thought* were beyond his powers. He has spoken freely and been transformed.

Quickly, the transformation process catches on, and Keating's students appear to be on fire with enthusiasm and ambition, ready to dance, play music, chant, beat drums, make love, run breathless and eager into the possibilities of the night. They seem, too, to have bonded as a team with a common purpose—to defy oppressive authorities and to experience life to the fullest.

In short, they intend to embody poetry's aim, as Keating has revealed it to them: "to suck the marrow out of life." Most important, the boys embrace that purpose as homage to their leader, whom they've taken to calling "Captain my Captain" (another Whitman line) and for whom they feel an obvious love and allegiance.

It is precisely at this point that things start to go terribly wrong. Discovering why will reveal some very important leadership lessons.

On that first day of classes, Keating decries the armies of academics who destroy poetry with pedantry, awakens his class to the dangers of their administration, and stirs them to a fever pitch of energy. The problem is that Keating provokes defiance without coalition, rebellion without acknowledgment of the social discourse necessary for true change. Keating's stance appears to be a bit too much of a performance; as Robert Heilman argues in an article on the film, "As a performer, he prefers role to program, attitude to the complexities of understanding."[4] The boys are stirred to act but have been rallied only to a vague cause of self-assertion that leaves them groping to create their own acts of rebellion in order to feel the coursing of their new blood: make a pass at another boy's girlfriend, forge a signature on a letter, disrupt a school assembly with a schoolboy prank, toss a desk set off the dormitory roof, gather in a nearby cave to read. They are becoming small-scale anarchists. Keating, however, pulls his punches, limiting his own rebellion to trivialities like ripping out book pages, parading in the school courtyard, and verbally jousting with a colleague over supper. His call to action is grand, his own actions curiously mannered.

## A Leadership Paradox

Maybe that is because, as Keating reveals to his students, he believes transformations are best kept secret. The secrecy of the mission is, supposedly, part of its romance. But it will also create an inescapable—and fatal—paradox for his students, who can't quite figure out how to be open in their identity and secret in their *pursuit* of identity. Equally difficult will be the task of openly supporting one another's aims without exposing one another's plans for achieving them. How to resolve this conflict? Eager to go to war without a weapon, the boys begin to lie. Keating has never intended for the boys to lie; but from the first huddle, where he distinguishes poetry over all other pursuits, he sets his class not only apart from others but above others as well. He poises them to "be like gods," and secrecy, Keating implies, is part of the ecstasy of discovering one's godlike self, though he omits the truth that a god must inevitably go public:

NEIL     What's the Dead Poets Society?

KEATING   I doubt the present administration would look too favorably upon that . . . can you keep a secret?

BOYS     Sure!

KEATING   The Dead Poets were dedicated to "sucking the marrow out of life." That's a phrase from Thoreau we would invoke at the beginning of every meeting. See, we would gather at the old Indian cave and take turns reading from Thoreau, Whitman, Shelley. The biggies. Even some of our own verse. And in the enchantment of the moment, we'd let poetry work its magic.

KNOX   You mean it was a bunch of guys sitting around reading poetry?

KEATING   No, Mr. Overstreet. It wasn't just "guys." We weren't a Greek organization. We were Romantics. We didn't just read poetry. We let it drip from our tongues like honey. Spirits soared. Women swooned. And gods were created, gentlemen. Not a bad way to spend an evening, eh? Thank you, Mr. Perry, for this stroll down amnesia lane. [pointing to yearbook] Burn that! Especially my picture!

As the boys become more and more excited about claiming the power of their identities, they are forced into more direct confrontation with the authorities they resent. The secrets slip out; the lies are recognized. The problem of being called to arms without the provision of specific tactics creates a troubling chaos. When one of Keating's students adds to the chaos by staging a "phone call from God" during a school assembly,

Keating is finally required to distinguish between daring and
foolishness.

KEATING    That was a pretty lame stunt you pulled today.

CHARLIE    You're siding with Mr. Nolan? What about
           Carpe diem? And sucking all the marrow out of
           life and all that?

KEATING    Sucking all the marrow out of life doesn't mean
           choking on the bone. See, there's a time for dar-
           ing, and there is a time for caution, and a wise
           man understands which is called for.

CHARLIE    But I thought you'd like that!

KEATING    No. You being expelled from school is not dar-
           ing to me. It's stupid. Because you'll miss some
           golden opportunities.

CHARLIE    Yeah? Like what?

KEATING    Like if nothing else, the opportunity to attend
           *my* classes. Got it, Ace?

CHARLIE    Aye aye, Captain.

KEATING    Keep your head about you. That goes for the
           lot of you.

BOYS       Yes, Captain!

KEATING    A phone call from God! If it had been collect?
           *That* would have been daring.

Which brings us to Keating's final flaw as a leader: he has inspired the boys to love him and to do as he advises, but he has not really helped them to understand the work itself.

Why stay in school? To be with Keating! He seems to be at the center of his subject—and of his students' admiration—more often than the poetry he teaches. Poetry in Keating's classroom, the very purpose of his leadership, is served up primarily as one-liners, terrific catchphrases that may ignite a ready heart but never provoke a genuine look into the deeper meanings of "the biggies" or into ways of applying their poetry to the difficult obstacles of living.

The greatest tragedy in *Dead Poets Society* is the suicide of one of Keating's best—and most confused—students, Neil Perry (Robert Sean Leonard). Neil loves Tennyson's verse "to strive, to seek, to find, and not to yield," but Keating never leads the boy to an understanding of *how* not to yield. The poem has, in the end, only eluded Neil, except perhaps to suggest to him that one must be dead to embrace the philosophies of the dead.

## The Failed Promise of Heroic Leadership

Keating has failed to provide the most important benefit of effective leadership: meaning. Instead, he has provided his own charisma as a replacement for meaning, and while this may sustain his students' (and the audience's) affections, it cannot sustain their lives. In short, he has become a hero, but not a leader. No wonder the boys lift him above their heads, carrying him across the field in adoration while Beethoven's Ninth Symphony, calling to mind its English chorus "Joyful, joyful, we adore thee, God of glory, Lord of love!", plays on the soundtrack. Keating is the golden hero, the valiant knight in shining armor who promises, but fails to deliver, their rescue. As Robert Heilman says, he has made a substitution of "personality for a decent discipline, of amiability for the instructional integrity that makes demands, of a subtle flattery for the more difficult task of assisting the young to grow up."[5] Keating's word appears to be golden as well, simply because it is *his*, and in this way his word becomes all too powerful. The power of Keating's word, spoken with compassion and kindness to the distraught Neil, pits Keating in direct and inescapable opposition to Neil's father. When Neil says, "I'm trapped," the sorry news is, he's right. He's trapped between two absolutes without being given any knowledge of how to navigate between them.

He abandons Tennyson's verse and "yields" by killing himself in his father's den; Keating is accused of negligence and abuse of power; and the boys are each bullied into copping pleas that guarantee Keating's dismissal. Although they've explored themselves, they've never been led toward any productive dialogue with the school, and must be overpowered. Inevitably, Keating is dismissed.

## A Failed Attempt to Seize the Day

Keating possessed much of the capacity to lead that is embodied in the poetry of the Romantics he so admired: focus on the individual over the group, the capacity for imagination, the visionary and transcendent experience. He revered originality and individuality as well as freedom and experimentation.

Yet he attempted to change a world ruled not by romantics, but by realists, people who possessed an unidealized view of life so different from his own—people who were detached, objective lovers of fact and rejecters of anything impractical. Successfully leading change requires a near-perfect balance of romanticism and practicality that Keating did not possess. As a result, he mistook heroism for effective leadership.

So, consider the final scene of *Dead Poets Society* in which the boys cry out to Keating as he makes his final, dramatic exit, "Oh Captain, my Captain!" The music swells; we are deeply moved. "Don't you forget this," Keating whispered to the shy Todd Anderson at the peak of their partnership. And Todd surely will not, nor will anyone who has seen this film. Heroism leaves an indelible impression, but what Keating has really *taught* is that in matters of leadership, love is not enough.

# PART TWO

# CREATING A TEAM

*Coach Norman Dale (Gene Hackman) commands loyalty through his far-reaching vision of success in* Hoosiers.

# FOUR

# Turning Around a Faltering Team

*Hoosiers*

### CAST OF CHARACTERS
Coach Norman Dale  *(Gene Hackman)*
Shooter  *(Dennis Hopper)*
Myra Fleener  *(Barbara Hershey)*
Cletus  *(Sheb Wooley)*

Director: David Anspaugh
Screenwriter: Angelo Pizzo

Almost everyone in the field house, which smells of varnish and sweat, is wearing a T-shirt emblazoned with the words "Go Milan Indians!" A Sousa march, wasted on a crowd already more than fully galvanized by the contest before them, blasts out of the public address system.

As a shot curves through the air, hits the side of the rim, rebounds off the backboard, and falls in, a fan yells, "Kill 'em, Indians! Kill 'em!" In the first row, center court, two cigar-chewing scouts earnestly compare notes that will later become reports to their clients and precursors to a scholarship at some Division I college. Outside, where several students sneak cigarettes and lean against cars decorated with crepe paper streamers and American flags, a muted cheer means a basket and pained groans mean a foul—or, worse, two points for the visitors.

It is the winter of 1954, and Milan (pronounced MY-lun) High, a Lilliputian southern Indiana school with only 161 students, has battled its way through the season's 751-team tournament to play the state powerhouse, Muncie Central, in the basketball finals. And these farm families who sit in the stands, proud that their high school basketball team—made up of dirt-poor, almost laughably short farm boys—has made it to the Indiana state championships. Their kids—1950s versions of today's Kevin Garnett, Kobe Bryant, and Tracy McGrady wannabes down there on the glistening parquet court—are heroes for a day, contenders in Indiana's version of the Super Bowl, the Kentucky Derby, Wimbledon, and The Masters, all wrapped into one.

There are just 18 seconds remaining in the game and the score is tied. Sportswriter William Gildea describes what is happening:[1]

The coach needs a shooter. He looks up confidently at the farm kid named Bobby Plump. The kid has played a mediocre game, but he's the one who led them all season. The plan is made: the ball will be thrown in to Plump and he will go one-on-one against his Muncie defender.

The team's center speaks up. He and three others should set up a "picket fence" on the left side of the court to lure the defense and give Plump almost the whole floor to work with. "Let's do that," says the coach. Plump will drive to the right and beat his man to the basket for a lay-up, or pull up and take the jump shot he learned as a boy on winter's frozen earth in southeastern Indiana.

Time in. Plump forgets the start of the play—by mistake, he throws the ball inbounds. But his backcourt partner returns the pass. The game is in Plump's hands. His teammates clear out. The slender boy with the crew cut in the black uniform with black knee-high socks dribbles out deep into the middle of the court. The seconds tick down. Seven, six, five . . .

Plump fakes left and drives right as he has done countless times in front of the backboard nailed to the family smokehouse. At precisely the right end of the

free-throw line he stops, jumps, and shoots. The ball
rips through the net. It's 32–30 in favor of Milan. The
final seconds expire. Milan is champion of all Indiana.

It was a moment made for movies, one that inspired basketball junkies David Anspaugh and Angelo Pizzo to make a
film called *Hoosiers* in 1986, its script based loosely on Milan
High's odyssey.

## An Outsider Comes to Town

In the film, set in Hickory, Indiana, before the opening of the
1951 season, Gene Hackman plays the Huskers' new coach Norman Dale, a man who hasn't been on a basketball court in more
than a decade. Dale has taken on an apparently impossible task:
replacing an irreplaceable coach. What's more, the team is
demoralized, caught in a streak of humiliating losses. A star
player has quit and retreated to the family farm, preferring self-
imposed isolation to celebrity. And the town of Hickory, suffering from a civic embarrassment it has never known before,
has lost its heart and its purpose.

In the midst of this melancholy, everybody seems to want
to run the basketball team. When, for example, Coach Dale
arrives in town, he is grilled by a group of good old boys down
at the barbershop. "This town doesn't like change much," one
of them begins, "so we thought we'd get together here tonight
and show you how we do things here." Another, a minister,
says: "We trust that you're a fine, upstanding, God-fearing man
with Christian morals and principles who will set an example

and a standard of leadership for our boys. Tell me, do you believe in man-to-man or a zone defense?"

This bizarre catechism turns downright menacing when George, the Huskers' former assistant coach, meets up with Coach Dale at the newcomer's first practice in Hickory High's gymnasium.

GEORGE Look, mister. These boys got a routine they're used to. You throw a new coach with newfangled ideas at 'em, might get 'em all confused. We'll ease into it real slow. Hell, our first game's less than two weeks away.

COACH DALE First of all, let's be real friendly here, OK? My name's Norm. Secondly, your coaching days are over.

GEORGE Look, mister. There's two kinds of dumb— the guy that gets naked and runs out in the snow and barks at the moon and the guy who does the same thing in my living room. First one don't matter. The second one you're kind of forced to deal with.

COACH DALE Translate. Is that some sort of threat?

GEORGE I don't know why [the principal] drug your tired old bones in here. He must've owed

you something fierce. Fact is, mister, you
start screwing up this team, I'll personally
hide-strap your ass to a pine rail and send
you on up the Monon line.

Can the game of basketball—or any game, for that
matter—fuel this kind of behavior? Absolutely. Sport is a kind
of microcosm of our society, mirroring how we compete, the
rules we go by, the values we hold. They're all there in the sta-
dium for us to see: the desire to succeed, a passion for competition, reverence for hard work, belief in progress and a brighter
tomorrow, a sense that only the fittest survive, and—perhaps
paradoxically—our desire to conform. (Sport, after all, is governed by rules and sanctions designed to discourage the very
individual freedoms democracy values.)

And although almost any sport, from alpine skiing to wu
shu, can serve well as a model for leaders and leadership, basketball is our sport of choice. Why? First, because basketball is
one of the most popular sports in the world, played by men
and women of all ages and ability levels in more than 200 countries. And, second, because it was created with one purpose in
mind: to change people.

Basketball, it turns out, was specifically designed by reform-
ers—its creator was a lapsed Christian minister given to
migraines—to guide American youth through the travails of
primary and secondary education. Basketball was a game with
a moral purpose, a direct descendant of the late-nineteenth-
century "Muscular Christian" movement, which held that society's ills could be cured through physical fitness. The idea was

that there might be more effective ways of doing good than preaching.

Basketball was not only perfectly suited to the YMCA's wholesomely Midwestern motto *mind, body, spirit*, but would soon be called the "city game" because of its popularity among urban youth. It had no pretensions.

How could it? After all, it was a sport named for the half-bushel peach baskets nailed to the balcony walls, a populist sport requiring a backboard to keep overly enthusiastic fans from deflecting the ball into the basket. And, as if to ensure that the game not be taken *too* seriously, the marvelously named *dribble* was invented, a move that—as an early rulebook breezily put it—was created "in response to the need of getting some place when in possession of the ball." The dribble was followed quickly by the *double dribble*, which enabled a closely guarded player to "voluntarily lose possession of the ball and yet regain it shortly." (Those peach baskets, which had a tendency both to slope forward and to wear out quickly, were soon made more durable and equipped with a chain-driven trapdoor gizmo that enabled the ball to be popped out.)

All this innovation yielded not only a new game, but also a powerful metaphor, one that storytellers and filmmakers alike would later find irresistible. From the tawdry *No Bull: The Unauthorized Biography of Dennis Rodman* to former senator Bill Bradley's uplifting *Values of the Game*; from the urban documentary *Hoop Dreams* (1994) to the very funny athletes-as-hustlers *White Men Can't Jump* (1992), basketball, it seems, is the stuff of which good books—and movies— are made.

## The Importance of Trust

*Hoosiers* serves up all of the elements better than any. There's competition, obsession, skill, and strategy, a community vying for public success, and a team of raw talents just waiting for someone with a rock-hard agenda to lead them to victory. And then of course there's Gene Hackman cast as that leader, an actor whose mere presence onscreen consistently sings with confidence.

You want a leader? Get Hackman. Remember all those soaked dinner guests in *The Poseidon Adventure* (1972), sloshing through the quickly rising Atlantic and swinging from steam pipes in the ship's engine rooms to follow Hackman's lead to safety, a new god, and dry land? And what could be more unnerving than watching Hackman twist that image of sound leadership to slimy deviance in *Absolute Power* (1997), creating one of the most lascivious presidents on film? Whatever side he plays on, good or evil, Hackman is a guy people trust.

Which is exactly why he's the perfect choice to play Coach Dale, a man who transforms himself from a volatile, self-serving sport dictator into a mature and compassionate leader who ultimately changes others. In keeping with the original spirit of the game of basketball, the transformation he inspires in his team is personal, not simply athletic. And the result is a sports Cinderella story—a small-town team rising from the dust of its losses to become champions. But this is no easy metamorphosis. As an outsider, Norman Dale is in no position to win hearts. Everything about him announces his displacement and perpetual isolation.

More important, he's an outsider to the failing basketball team he's hired to coach; and, worse still, he's been kicked out of professional coaching for hitting a player. He has, it seems, been evicted from life.

But could Norman Dale's experience on the outside of just about everything be his ticket to success?

The idea that the burden of banishment, and all its implied lessons, can be used to a winning advantage, as Dale uses his, isn't new to sport movies. Harold Abrahams, played by actor Ben Cross in *Chariots of Fire* (1981), epitomized the outsider as victor in that Oscar-winning film about the 1924 Olympics. A Jewish student cast out of the academic and social community he covets, this athlete is determined to run a helluva lot faster and better than anyone—and, sure enough, he does. In that film, it is Harold's exile that prompts his race from an apparently unredeemed world. He epitomizes extraordinary separateness, authority, and power, that unique alchemy that has grabbed the attention of scholars, historians, theologians, philosophers, and psychologists for decades.

Few stories grab an audience like the story of the outsider who succeeds. For instance, in the lighter but no less revealing American film of W. P. Kinsella's classic baseball fantasy, *Field of Dreams* (1989), Kevin Costner plays an emotional loner. He's broke, washed up, breaking down, and tormented by a sense of professional and personal failure. He's lost his father, his farm, and his direction. What's he to do?

He bucks all the odds and builds a baseball field worthy of the greatest players in baseball history, the ghosts of whom show up with the ghost of his dead father to play a game of catch and to enact Kinsella's leadership catchphrase of the '80s, *If you build it, they will come.* And Spike Lee's spectacular high school basketball player Jesus Shuttlesworth, in 1998's *He Got Game,* is driven to success by a father who has fallen so far out of the game he's incarcerated in San Quentin.

The lesson in all of these films seems to be the same: the outsider is tough and determined, and hasn't got much to lose by pushing the boundaries of a vision that may become, in the end, a kind of professional, social, personal, even spiritual redemption. There's something invaluable, it seems, about being in the outer circle.

The sometimes-surprising effects of exile have also been revealed by studies of what makes certain groups outperform others. Joel Kotkin, who delved into this counterintuitive phenomenon while a Fellow at Pepperdine University, found, for example, that some of history's most frequently exiled groups were propelled by their ancient dispersion to do the seemingly impossible. Producing more billionaires, Nobel Prize winners, and gifted intellectuals per capita than most major European and East Asian countries, the children of the Diaspora, Kotkin writes, "developed a unique set of attitudes toward themselves and the world. In a pattern seen today most noticeably with the Japanese or Chinese, the Jews maintained a ferocious loyalty to their own identity even as their power reached its fullest expression through dispersion."[2] Whether you apply it to Mormons, Cubans, Palestinians, or Jews, Kotkin's intriguing and controversial research suggests that it is a group's separateness that, paradoxically, gives it its strength.

Exile, as Kotkin's study suggests, can become a crucible of pain, power, initiative, motive, and will. But it's important to appreciate the difference between the extreme position of the exiled and the position of the outsider. Although the two are similar, they aren't the same, as William Gass, winner of the National Book Award for Criticism, explains:

> To be exiled is not to be flung out of any door, but out of your own door; it is to lose your home, where home suggests a close personal belonging and the gnarled roots of one's identity. I cannot be exiled from café society because I never had a home there. I can be expelled from school, or ejected from the game, but I cannot be exiled from them.[3]

The exiled and outsiders are thrown different directions from different doors, but these groups share vital outlooks, as well as tools for responding to a sudden, unwanted displacement. What *Hoosiers* adds to all of this is an understanding of the more complex meaning and function of displacement, of not being on the team, and its relationship to teambuilding.

Dale uses his own background and savvy as an outsider in several unexpected ways, becoming a kind of expert reader of individual loss and isolation—a skill that will help him create a stellar team and to lead it to victory.

## Who's on the Inside?

If an individual or a group is on the outside, there are certainly some people or groups who think they're in. And in *Hoosiers*, the folks in Hickory, Indiana, seem to know exactly who's in and who's out. The ballplayers, of course, are considered the central insiders—a bunch of cocky kids, suddenly fumbling without a coach, used to calling all the shots themselves, with no experience in basketball fundamentals and defense.

Then there are the townspeople, all of them certain of their insider status, ready to bully Dale. Add to this a couple of compelling loners, qualified insiders who prefer to watch from the sidelines: Jimmy, a star talent who's "backed away from pretty much everything," and Shooter (Dennis Hopper), the drunk who nevertheless "knows everything there is to know about the greatest game ever invented."

These are the facts, according to majority view. But Dale sees things quite differently. What follows is a bizarre series of maneuvers on Dale's part that leave everyone wondering, How far out *is* this guy?

He rejects group meetings; insults the town that is hosting him; and throws talented kids off the team, or benches them, or won't let them shoot baskets, speak, smile, or, it seems, win. He's constantly in verbal battles with his opposition, provokes others, gets kicked out of games, refuses to recruit a star player, and instead recruits the town drunk. Norman Dale doesn't seem to know anything about "managing multiple constituencies." Simply translated, it looks like Dale can't get along with other people. No wonder it seems he'll be the man on the outside of the team, and the town, forever.

## Who's *Really* on the Inside?

Nobody. And Dale knows it.

Dale acts with the knowledge that, in Hickory, there is no

inside, no outside, and no real team—only the fantasy of one, a bunch of enthusiastic, inexperienced people who get together, throw ideas at impossible baskets, and have fun planning for their unlikely success. The Hickory Huskers, in other words, are anything but a team. They have become, instead, isolated and vulnerable. They have lost the identity and satisfaction that comes to human beings through authentic group membership. They have become a pseudo-team, a kind of dysfunction not uncommon in business organizations where a misguided view of teams can too easily turn into the quick-fix blunder.

At Levi Strauss & Co., for example, a well-intentioned management recently did away with the piecework system, an out-of-date procedure forcing seamstresses, for example, to install as many pockets as they could each day. In its place, the company's gurus established teams, groups of workers whose wages depended on the total number of jeans they produced. According to an article in the *Wall Street Journal*, executives thought the idea was sound. Work would be less boring, each employee could be cross-trained to do other tasks, morale would improve. As one executive rhapsodized, "This change will lead to a self-managed work environment that will reduce stress and help employees become more productive."[4]

He could not have been more wrong. The management's well-intentioned attempt to empower its factory workers created pseudo-teams destined to create more problems than they solved. Speedy seamstresses found themselves victim to the lowest common denominator—their slower colleagues. Morale plummeted. Quality and efficiency reached new lows, while labor and overhead costs increased dramatically.

Lower-skilled workers' pay increased while their more productive counterparts' decreased. Such inequities led one unhappy stitcher to say publicly what many were feeling: "I hate teams. Levi's is not the place it used to be."

Like many organizations, the town of Hickory, Indiana, has a misguided view of teams, and does not recognize that it has become just a collection of disparate, disorganized people suffering a fear of teamlessness and loneliness.

Only Dale can see the truth. And he will focus keenly on these "island selves" around him, figure out just what everyone is missing, determine exactly why each individual has come to feel disconnected (like an outsider) and then begin to repair the losses and disconnections he discerns. Once he initiates that damage control, his team will come together with a real psychic strength that for other teams may only be pretense.

## What Don't They Have?

While many leadership experts suggest recognizing what individuals have, Dale effectively recognizes what the individuals around him *don't* have, a far more likely and powerful lever for motivating individual and group behaviors.

He might have studied Abraham Maslow's hierarchy of needs at the Harvard Business School. Lest you've forgotten your Management 101 class, it was Maslow who, while pondering what makes people tick, came up with the attractively simple idea that we're all driven by just five basic needs:

- physiological (life necessities like food)
- safety

- love and belonging (affection, acceptance from others)
- esteem (self-respect and respect from others)
- self-actualization (self-fulfillment and reaching one's potential)

Fair enough. But what made this notion really exciting was Maslow's theory that it's what's missing in our lives that drives us, and furthermore that these needs are hierarchical. Simply put, until we've satisfied our more basic needs—a living wage, for example—the more important ones don't even appear on our motivational radar. Hence, it'll take more than a pat on the back to motivate an employee who can't make a mortgage payment.

Dale is able to discern what's missing from his player's lives, and offers real, not conceptual, solutions. And he has the guts to use radical, unpopular methods for creating the needed, genuine core team, one that all of Hickory's "island selves" can count on.

## Establishing the Inside

Dale's first step is to publicly reject the opinion that he is an outsider at all. Should he sit around negotiating with those barbershop boys? He could. But instead, Dale walks out—not the number-one suggestion on a traditional tip sheet for the new guy on the team. But by talking, Dale would send the wrong message: *I want to be let in, please.* By walking, he says instead: *I* am *in.* You *are out!* Suddenly, the new guy in town has taken charge by creating his own boundaries. Next, he clarifies those boundaries to the basketball team, the Huskers. To create for them a clear sense of being the new insiders, Dale lets them know the team is now a private organization based upon new laws.

How? Ostracism.

The idea of using ostracism in any modern society to establish a standard or policy is not a crowd-pleaser, and in most hierarchies it's downright offensive—but Dale is more than willing to try it. He throws a defiant player out of a practice within minutes and repeatedly benches a smart aleck for violating team agreement, even at the expense of losing. Just as a business might withhold promotions and raises from employees who are unwilling to embrace company policies or practices—and who as a result become outsiders—Dale withholds membership to his basketball team.

His praise becomes the equivalent of a desired promotion— "Those of you there on the floor at the end? I'm proud of you"—and is pointedly exclusive.

## Creating Insider Solidarity

Dale does an awful lot of yelling. He seems to have no diplomacy, no sense of tact. It may be a cutthroat game, but he seems out of control, perhaps on the brink of another "incident" like the one that ended his early career.

This time, though, there is a method to his madness. By verbally assaulting his opponents—calling them "a bunch of gorillas," vociferously defending his team inside "this cage you call a gym"—Dale achieves two goals: he establishes his protectiveness of the team (remember those boundaries); and he identifies a looming threat, a hostile *other* against whom the boys may struggle, a key component in the achievement of team loyalty.

In this way he reaches his most difficult team player, who leaps to Dale's defense during an on-court squabble. "I got him good, didn't I, Coach?" is the boy's overexcited announcement that he has joined the team by demonstrating unequivocally that he's ready to defend those boundaries. He's in.

## Recognizing Loss

The catalyst for Dale's arrival is the loss of the former coach. And the team has lost a lot of games. But it is important to distinguish between the *literal loss* experienced by your team— games or coaches—and the far-reaching *sense of loss* that results. Dale is navigating an enormous sea of losses, which give precise form to his leadership principles. Certainly he knows how loss motivates—he's lost his career, his path, and his ticket to the world he loves, and he wants it all back. Like other characters in *Hoosiers*, Dale recalls the moment his own life changed:

> COACH DALE I can't really explain that. It's been a number of years, it still kinda goes around in my head. I slow it down, sometimes I really think that I can stop my fist from hitting that boy's jaw. In one second, everything I worked for was just all finished.

Now he can apply what he's learned from his own life as he strengthens his team. He begins by gathering information, collecting and absorbing details about the losses suffered by his players and in fact by everyone he meets. He ends up with an encyclopedic catalog of loss.

• Jimmy, the star player, has lost a father figure (the former coach), his own father, his mother, and his freedom to choose for himself.
• The boys on the team have lost their confidence and their self-respect.
• Everett, Shooter's son, has lost respect for his alcoholic father.
• Myra, Jimmy's guardian, has lost her father and must deal with her mother's illness.
• The townspeople have lost their pride.
• Shooter has lost a son's respect and, years ago, a basketball game, a crippling failure.

Dale amiably invites more information, as in the exchange with the tough-as-nails Myra (Barbara Hershey):

COACH DALE    So what are you doing here? Living in Hickory?

MYRA    I haven't always been here. I went to college three years. Graduate school a year.

COACH DALE    Graduate school!

MYRA    Surprised? You sound like my father. He thought it strange I ever wanted to leave

town. Kept telling me I'd be back. Of
course he was right.

COACH DALE  Why'd you come back?

MYRA  It didn't work out. Daddy died. Mother got
sick. I had to come back.

COACH DALE  You never plan on leaving? Did you ever
consider getting married? Come on! You
must've had a lot of opportunities!

## Recognizing Effects

After collecting all this information, Dale then keenly observes
the behavior that has resulted from these losses: uncommu-
nicativeness (Jimmy), belligerence (Rade), anger (Rade, Everett,
Myra), self-deprecation (Ollie, Shooter), arrogance (Rade, the
barbershop boys), possessiveness (Myra and the townspeople),
hysteria (the townspeople), and confusion (everyone) all the
elements of a disintegrating whole that obstruct team performance and unity.

## Holding Out the Carrot

Using a variety of approaches and demeanors, Dale offers
people a game plan for obtaining that thing they miss the most.
His team will come together gradually as individuals work
toward what they need and abandon the behaviors that stand
in their way.

Coach Dale's approach to Shooter is particularly illustrative of this:

COACH DALE    I want you to be my assistant. I want you to come to practices and sit on the bench with me during games.

SHOOTER       Me? You want me?

COACH DALE    Whaddya say? Under the following conditions. That you clean yourself up, and you shave, and you show up at the games on time, and at practices, and you wear a shirt and tie.

SHOOTER       Oh, I got myself a suit. Right there. I got a wingdinger! I married in that suit!

COACH DALE    And that you're sober.

SHOOTER       Oh no. My wife sent you. My son. What has my drinking got to do with my knowledge about basketball?

COACH DALE    You can't drink in front of these boys. If I smell even a trace of liquor on your breath, you'd be finished.

Gradually, Dale is building a team by making deals. And he is working with people beyond his core team, initiating a wide variety of bargains to improve his team, and in the process the community.

Dale's explicit bargains are the raw material of transactional leadership, a kind of simple cost-benefit exchange process between leader and follower. It's an economist's dream and marvelously simple. The basic idea is for the leader to find ways to compensate when the subordinate's job or environment fails to motivate, an idea that nicely complements those hierarchical needs we mentioned earlier. In its simplest manifestation, this means subordinates get a bonus when they achieve an assigned goal, just as Shooter will get a job if he cleans up and stops drinking. Or, subordinates tidily do what's expected, relying on the calculus of the transaction: you do this for me, and I'll do that for you.

## Giving Freedom

The approach is not always so clear-cut. What should he do, for instance, with Jimmy? Here's a guy who poses an interesting challenge. He seems to have it all, and what he doesn't have— a team, a new coach—he doesn't seem to want. He doesn't want to transform himself; why bother, when you're at the top of the heap? What kind of deal can be made with a player so solid in his identity as a star that *he* seems to be the one with all the bargaining power, power that he will use when the moment is ripe? It's no surprise that everyone is all over this kid and his bright future. Seems like the only thing Jimmy *doesn't* have is control of his own decisions.

In one short scene with Jimmy, Norman Dale reveals his deepest principle as a leader: every player owns his talent, and is his own team. By giving a clear signal of individual liberty to a player who has lost all self-government just by virtue of being everybody's hero, Dale creates the unthreatening, attractive environment Jimmy needs:

COACH DALE  You know, in the ten years that I coached, I never met anybody who wanted to win as badly as I did. I'd do anything I had to do to increase my advantage. Anybody who tried to block the pursuit of that advantage, I'd just push 'em out of the way, it didn't matter who they were, or what they were doing there. But that was then. You've got a special talent. A gift. It's not the school's. Not the townspeople. Not the team's. Not Myra Fleener's. Not mine. It's yours, to do with what you choose. Because that's what I believe, I can tell you this—I don't care if you play on the team or not.

And because he really *means* this, and is not acting for gain, Dale seems as surprised as everyone else when Jimmy shows up at a town meeting to bargain on Dale's behalf and join the team. "I play, Coach stays. He goes, I go." This is a star finally in full possession of his lost power.

There's no art of the deal here, no transaction, no quid pro quo. Just laserlike and unconditional focus on what really counts—Jimmy's ownership of and responsibility for his own talent and potential. Such transformational leadership creates not only a strong personal identification with and emotional attachment to the leader, but also a new level of independence for the follower. The result? Jimmy now understands better than ever the purpose and mission of the team and is ready to work for the good of the group. Coach Dale has created a new vision for Jimmy that transforms him.

This is complex, but not magic. Coach Dale has simply combined transactional leadership with transformational leadership, artfully building the latter on the foundation of the former. In addition to this, he has modeled four leadership behaviors that are fundamental to effective teambuilding and are confirmed by research into the nature of transformational leadership.[5]

First, Dale has used *charisma*, providing not only a vision but also a sense of mission and pride. He's gained Jimmy's respect and trust. He has also succeeded in getting Jimmy to identify with him.

Second, he's *inspired* Jimmy. He's become an exemplar and model. But whereas charisma requires identification with the leader, inspiration does not.

Third, Dale helps Jimmy achieve his fullest potential by *providing individual consideration*. Part coaching and part mentoring, such consideration ensures that a follower receives continuous feedback that links his or her needs to the organization's mission.

Finally, Dale provides *intellectual stimulation*. He's presented Jimmy with a series of challenging new ideas that will cause Jimmy to rethink his old ways of doing things.

The result of all of this is that Jimmy is aware, perhaps for the first time, of his own beliefs and values. Only now can he be ready to generate new solutions that he's never dreamed of before.

## The Team Recovers

What are the results of Dale's radical, and personal, techniques? A loyal, expert, and fulfilled team that has directly addressed the errors and behaviors that have cost it success. By virtue of strong foundations, which were built from the rubble of loss, a team established on such principles should be able to survive even the loss of its leader, which Dale insists on proving to the team by removing himself from a game, despite Shooter's pleas, "You got to give me your word that you will not be kicked out of no games!"

Consider this: when the founder and director of the Williamstown Theatre Festival, Nikos Psacharopoulos, was approached by a board of trustees requesting a leadership game plan before his death, he adamantly refused to provide one. Though the success of his company was in many ways directly related to his leadership vision and to his ability to establish a team that was both exclusive and warmly inclusive, he shrugged at the idea of mapping out his vision for the company's future. His reasoning was simple: "If I built it strong, then it will go on—without my game plan."

What made Psacharopoulos's leadership both eccentric and powerful was his belief that his singular vision did not have to last—only the powerful core structure that would allow new talents to thrive after his exit.

Who knows, at the end of *Hoosiers*, if Coach Dale is around or not? But we do know that there's a kid shooting baskets on that court, looking up at a photograph of the team that is his inspiration. Something has been passed along. Dale's own basketball team, of course, has disbanded, many of the boys gone on to college—but the Huskers will continue to draw a team and a crowd.

The proof? By the end of this film, Coach Dale's team has expanded to draw in the entire town, largely thanks to a leader with a keen understanding of what it means to be on the outside.

And his team's new inclusiveness is proof not only of his success as a leader, but of the unifying thrill for people who have recovered their losses. This is when Dale's methods and far-reaching, compassionate vision of team potential starts to look a lot like healing.

*Norma Rae (Sally Fields) emerges as a leader with a clear and compelling message in* Norma Rae.

# FIVE

# MENTORS AND PROTÉGÉS

## *Norma Rae*

### CAST OF CHARACTERS

Norma Rae  *(Sally Field)*

Reuben  *(Ron Leibman)*

Sonny  *(Beau Bridges)*

Vernon  *(Pat Hingle)*

Leona  *(Barbara Baxley)*

Director: Martin Ritt

Screenwriters: Irving Ravetch and Harriet Frank, Jr.

The 1979 film *Norma Rae*, one of the most popular pro-worker films ever made, is the fictionalized story of a Roanoke, Virginia, mill-hand named Crystal Lee Sutton. Sutton successfully took on the Patterson Textile Mill conglomerate as a union organizer in the 1970s, proving that extraordinary power doesn't have to depend on status or title. We witness the unmistakable development of leadership capacity in someone who seemed destined to always be a follower.

Norma Rae, at first dependent and repressed, becomes a charismatic leader who enables significant change to occur in the lives of her friends and coworkers, thanks to a successful mentor–protégée relationship that stirs enough human energy and will to reverse the grinding gears of an organization.

It's not the first time that factory workers have been portrayed as replaceable parts in the industrial machine. In the 1936 film classic *Modern Times*, we come face to face with the potential of such organizations to dominate workers' lives. There's the routine enforced by the clock: employees must arrive at a dictated time, and they must complete a predetermined amount of work before the day is done. Each shift is inexorably replaced by another at 8-hour intervals so the work can continue without interruption. The work itself is machinelike and incessant, and the workers—whether processing insurance applications in a gigantic "office factory" or forging engine blocks for automobiles—are just part of the machine, machines making machines.

Charlie Chaplin's wickedly funny satire of "modern" labor, *Modern Times*, portrays the Little Tramp's touching efforts to come to grips with the machine age. In its opening scene, a herd of sheep (a black one stands out) jostles in its pen, and then hurries across the screen, as if on its way to the slaughter-house; a dissolve then reveals a throng of hundreds of workers rushing similarly into a steel factory. Then Charlie, all dolled up in his signature derby, ill-fitted jacket, and cane, goes about his numbing business, tightening bolts on the parade of steel plates that arrive at his workstation. As the conveyor belt speeds faster and faster, he can't keep up, causing no end of trouble for his more agile coworkers. Later, he collapses onto the conveyor belt and is dragged into the cogs of the surrealistic assembly line's gearwheels. The metaphor is complete. The tramp has become, quite literally, part of the machinery. Finally, he goes berserk and destroys the factory, becoming, as one film wag has pointed out, a "nut" himself.

The unhappy fact, of course, is that the Little Tramp is not alone, nor is he an irrelevant anachronism. Once we start to keep pace *with* a machine, we become *part* of the machine.

Like the Little Tramp, Norma Rae (Sally Field) is powerless at first, a down-and-outer whose life is destined to be drab and insignificant. In fact, she is a person who has done very little in her life besides survive it. She has never called the main shots in anything. She is no breaker of glass ceilings, no pioneering trailblazer with even the slightest hope of changing things, and certainly not upwardly mobile. Under her direction, nothing has ever been restructured, dismantled, or built, no strategy created. She is a person whose fate seems sealed. She is a cog in the grand wheeling machine of the cotton mill in which she has worked for most of her life.

Fittingly, the movie starts with the eerie images of a textile mill spinning and humming away as though in no need of human energies and substance, then with a woman's face in still shots: Norma Rae in infancy, Norma Rae hugging a man, Norma Rae holding her own infant, and Norma Rae moving through her colorless life, the photographs suggest, without really moving at all. And over these images and the opening credits, we hear a singing voice that lets us know this isn't going to be easy viewing, but a sad and difficult journey.

No fresh young leaders bursting onto the scene, full of ideas and humor and applauded by their coworkers. You won't see anyone striding in with confidence, skill, and a ready plan of action, people who arrive on the screen as leaders fully formed, raring to go at their work with energy and, for the most part, pleasure.

This is a different sort of story altogether. In fact, the environment we're forced to face in the first several minutes of *Norma Rae* leads us to believe that there may be no success story here at all.

## In the Maw of the Machine

The O. P. Henley Textile Mill, employing over 800 nonunionized workers, couldn't be more oppressive. The noise is horrendous; the hours are long and sometimes longer, depending on the whim of management; there are no windows; there are only short, useless breaks. There is no escaping the building or the job, as there is no other work in town, and the place is patrolled by slave drivers who make the mill look like the appalling work camp it is.

Enter Norma Rae. She starts off only with an unmanageable rebelliousness that's made her a wild girl around town, and with an unused intelligence she doesn't even know is hers. She'll have to learn and discover herself as she goes; she'll have to work always from the lowest level of the organization; and she'll need to team up with an experienced leader, an outsider, a mentor— the urban, crass union representative Reuben Warshofsky (Ron Leibman). This insider and outsider will become protégée and mentor and forge a successful team. Where do they begin?

Consider this protégée in her early career. Norma Rae is one tough cookie. She's already got management eyeing her for her pouting demands and fiery accusations, and, unlike her coworkers, she confronts her bosses when she's good and mad. Her energy is unharnessed. She doesn't yet know the real power behind her anger. Interestingly, her bosses at the mill do, and they try to shut her up quickly.

How? By promoting her and offering her the raise they know she—like all the others—needs so badly. They know they've got a coltish leader in the making, a ground shaker, and they'd better get her out of action fast with the promise of cash in hand.

Norma Rae does take the promotion, but she doesn't keep it for long—not when it separates her from the only community she's got, her coworkers. Here's an important truth about Norma Rae that will define her leadership later: she finds strength with others. She's an insider through and through, and she'd rather work on the inside than become a high-level outcast. Instinctively she chooses the power she finds in the group, not the power of position. Fortunately, Norma Rae's bosses aren't the only ones to notice her potential for power. When outsider and soon-to-be mentor Reuben arrives in town, he is told by everyone he's come to defend to "shove off, get off, and go away!" This union recruiter needs to cast his net for an insider, someone to legitimize his goals from within the organization.

## Building Alliances

Like management consultants who regularly parachute in to bring order out of chaos at ailing companies, Reuben's first and most important task is to find a collaborator, someone who can work on the inside. Such insider-outsider combinations succeed. Consider how stodgy old Sears, for example, has recently begun to put retail powerhouse Wal-Mart on the run. The key was not just Sears's CEO Arthur Martinez's widely publicized decision to hire the change wizards at A. T. Kearney, a top consulting firm, to help him turn the ailing retail giant around. It was also the adroit way in which he combined the efforts of these hired infiltrators with trusted insiders at Sears.

While the Kearney outsiders were ordered to scour the place for ways to cut costs, Martinez simultaneously got his trusted lieutenants on the inside to focus on how to grow revenues. These newly revved-up insiders went so far as to set up Nevada Bob's golf shops in Sears's archaic sporting goods departments and to create Sears Home Services with thousands of service workers who work in customers' homes. The result of this insider-outsider collaboration blend has been impressive. Sears's share price has lately outperformed such winners as Coca-Cola, Disney, and IBM.

Martinez brought in his consultants, and Reuben brings in Norma Rae. Maybe Reuben knows, with solid instinct, that Norma Rae may not be a surefire bet, but she's the only bet he's got. He needs a dialogue with a worker. He also needs someone poised to fight.

Reuben gains Norma Rae's trust by gently but assertively offering her a vision of herself that is completely new to her—a vision of her own strength, intelligence, and the potential to turn her fiery temperament toward an organized battle. He allows her to mentor him. It's a phenomenon we call *reverse mentoring*, in which the protégée is encouraged to guide her mentor. This unique relationship has an instant and productive result. When she points out that his union flyer has "too many big words! If I don't understand it, they ain't gonna understand it!" he rewrites it and tells her, "I took your advice." He lets her know she can help him, as much as he can help her, and his invitation that she focus on her potential is both urgent and caring. And when Norma Rae shows up at his union organization meeting with some other workers, he gives her a final, confidential push: "If I don't get some help soon, I'm outta here, and you've got nothing."

Norma Rae chooses to enter the fray as a fledgling leader and is guided by Reuben through all of the hazards of learning to lead as you go along. The initial courtship of mentor and protégée has ended, and the harder work of partnership has begun for both of them. Not only do they have to take on several tasks at once—outmaneuvering all the obstacles thrown in their path, drumming up enthusiasm for their cause in the midst of hostility, recruiting workers, distributing information, creating the necessary army of union supporters while time passes them by much too quickly—they also have to admit to their mutual flaws and mentor each other.

It's important to remember that although Reuben is the experienced leader, the obvious mentor, he needs Norma Rae as much as she needs him. For the partnership to work, Reuben must be Norma Rae's student as well as her teacher. While Norma Rae is enthusiastic and warm, a real "people" leader as she encourages others to join the cause, she has a harder time learning the difficult balance of authority and compassion, the power of confrontation, and the necessity of a pinch of personal risk. Reuben is there to "spot-check" her.

## The Magic of a Mentor

It's doubtful that Norma Rae could succeed without Reuben's help. In his classic study of leaders, *On Heroes and Hero Worship*, the nineteen-century writer Thomas Carlyle asserted that "Most humans are as kindling, waiting for the match to ignite them." Reuben *is* that match, even though he is the consummate outsider. With his heavy Bronx accent and Yiddish idiom, his looks, and his manner, this mensch and mentor seems to the folks in Henleyville like he's from another planet. But he's a wise, trustworthy counselor and teacher, the perfect adviser for Norma Rae. Reuben will, to colloquialize Carlyle's point, light her fire.

Reuben *is* Mentor, and just as his ancient predecessor changed everything for Odysseus's son Telemachus, so too does Reuben ignite a transformation in his protégée, Norma Rae. Reuben is an intellectual friend, a *kibitzer*, someone who's been there and done that with some good intentions; someone who watches, listens, prods, criticizes, and often provokes. His success, it turns out, will be her success.

Reuben knows every twist and turn of the legal system that can work in his favor, plus how to use what he knows as a strong weapon of defense *and* offense. But he's pushy, too often says the right things in the wrong way, and has trouble connecting with others from his outsider's position.

Here's Reuben's "letter of the law" approach, appropriate for confrontation and for maintaining authority against opposition as he inspects the mill:

REUBEN    [In front of bulletin board] Somebody's looking to get into a carpool. Somebody wants to sell a basset pup. And you can pick pecans for 40 cents a bushel. Isn't that terrific. The only thing that's missing is my notice.

BOSS    It's there.

REUBEN    It is? I don't see it. [Boss points to top of bulletin board] Oh, yes! Wilt Chamberlain on stilts could read that thing, maybe. Wanna bring it down to eye level, brothers, where everybody can read it?

BOSS    We'll make note of your request.

REUBEN    Why do you guys pull this horseshit, huh? Now I have to go to the phone, call my lawyers, and get 'em on your ass. That's childish. All right. Where's the pay phone and who's got two nickels?

BOSS    Hey, Vic. Bring it down.

REUBEN    To eye, eye level, eye.

BOSS      You ain't supposed to read the damn thing.

REUBEN    No union or organizer, not even a known union
          member, has been inside the fences or walls of
          this factory for more than ten years. I'm readin'
          it.

BOSS      Well read fast then.

REUBEN    All right, I'll tell you what. While I'm reading
          this, you go read the court order that says any
          agent of this company can be held in contempt.
          You're messin' with a contempt citation, so if
          you're hot for jail, you just keep it up.

BOSS      I ain't violatin' no law.

REUBEN    You're violatin' the law right now, baby!

BOSS      Are we finished here?

REUBEN    Certainly. Where's the other bulletin board?

BOSS      In the weaving room.

REUBEN    You wanna show it to me?

BOSS      Yes. Hell. Yes.

Norma Rae, on the other hand, has those great people skills,
an insider's authority, and no understanding of the law, or of
organized oppositional leadership. Alone, these two will get
nowhere. Together, their different styles create the vigor, concern, and authority necessary for influencing others.

Weaving their styles together, Norma Rae and Reuben will keep piping up with tips for one another—what to say, what to read, when to "get them legally," when to confront—and with requests for help.

Here's a tip for Reuben from Norma Rae:

REUBEN    I'm not getting the message across. [We've got] 17 out of 800?

NORMA RAE    Well. You're an outsider. Things move slow around here. This isn't New York, where you grab a taxi and your hat.

REUBEN    You got any ideas?

NORMA RAE    Yeah. Buy a jug of corn whiskey and meet me here on Saturday. We're gonna hit the backroads.

## Reverse Mentoring

What's going on here? Can the student possibly be teaching the mentor?

You bet. This is no rebellious role reversal, no protégée gone pushy. Instead, it's the kind of give-and-take that can transform the sometimes bland and potentially domineering relationship that develops between mentor and protégé into something that is fluid, democratic, and near magical. Norma Rae's reverse mentoring of Reuben delivers an important leadership truth: Leaders sometimes—no, frequently!—follow, and they learn.

And followers, even those lowest on the organizational totem pole, often lead and teach.

"The writing is on the wall for the technophobic, old-style thinking boomers," writes Don Tapscott, chair of the Alliance for Convergent Technologies. "Unless they throw out years of conditioning and old models of work, they will be washed away by a tsunami of media-savvy, confident, peer-oriented, innovative N-Geners, i.e., the 'Net Generation.' Call it generational displacement in the workforce. For traditionalist, die-hard boomers, this is going to bring a whole new meaning to the term early retirement."[1] The message? Get going and learn from the kids. And successful companies are finally beginning to get this message. In 1994, for instance, a diversity forum at Procter & Gamble developed a reverse-mentoring program called Mentor Up that helps senior managers learn from younger employees, mostly women.

Think of it this way: In any organization or community not run by tyrants, leaders and followers—like Reuben and Norma Rae—continually pass the leadership baton back and forth. Each learns from the other. Each teaches the other. As W. F. Foster, who studied leaders and their followers, puts it, the relationship becomes a "conjunction of ideas where leadership is shared and transferred between leaders and followers, each only a temporary designation. Indeed, history will identify an individual as the leader, but in reality the job is one in which various members of the community contribute. Leaders and followers are interchangeable."[2] Increasingly, we know that leadership no longer responds to the law of gravity. It can, in fact, and frequently should, go up as well as down.

Reuben's occasional transformation from teacher to critic is instructive. The better Norma Rae gets at leading, the higher he raises the bar. "Mouthy," he says, "you're too muscular. You can't come down that hard on a man and leave him his balls. Easy! Jesus. If you were in the State Department, we'd be at war."

Mentors not only nurture and support, they also administer tough love when needed. That's because mentoring is not solely an altruistic undertaking—it's also about results. Denis Boyles, who has studied the behavior of mentors, explains this tendency to deftly combine punishment with reward. "Protégés are protégés because their mentors believe that by making them protégés, they will increase their own worth. The downside: If making you a protégé becomes less than cost-efficient, you're outta there pronto. This kind of relationship is all business, after all."[3]

Such advice-giving is becoming important as a career development tool, particularly for women. It is estimated that over 90 percent of women executives have had mentors sometime in their careers and that, of those, 80 percent consider their mentors to be important to their career advancement.

But of course, this isn't limited to women. Over 96 percent of Fortune 500 executives—most of whom are men—credited mentoring as an important influence in the development of their professional lives. There is, apparently, nothing like a guide when it comes to plotting out that next career move. "Sometimes you can get lost climbing the corporate ladder and need someone to help navigate the maze," said one protégé who had been helped by his mentor, a senior executive at financial services giant Bank of America. At Burlington Northern Santa Fe

Railway Company, formally appointed mentors cram more than two years' of work experience into their charges in just six monthly meetings.

The bottom line is that, even in this age of galloping entrepreneurialism, becoming an effective leader is as much a matter of human reciprocity as it is a solo act. You can benefit greatly from someone else's experience. And his or her knowledge can yield important career rewards like salary, promotion, job satisfaction, power, and influence. Playing protégé to a first-class mentor is a sure way to learn the organizational ropes.

## Building Relationships

But there's more here than the story of a young woman making it in an antediluvian sweatshop in the hills of Virginia. *Norma Rae*'s subtext is about the ever-changing relationship between two people. This relationship proceeds from suspicious curiosity and distinct distrust to a symbiotic cooperation built on the belief that mutual goals are both important and achievable. And when the alliance has developed fully, Reuben and Norma Rae become a force to be reckoned with, an unbeatable team. As a result, you just know that things are going to change down at the mill.

The development of such power has been the subject of a great deal of research. One study, for instance, found that there are two primary developmental phases in a healthy mentoring relationship.[4] It all starts, it seems, with something akin to a mating ritual. This phase of the mentor-protégé relationship is called *initiation*, and it begins the moment the mentor and the protégé first discover each other. They size each other up, take each other's measure, to get a sense of each other's style and work habits. They test each other, probe for the possibility of an alliance.

The goal? To discover if there is an opportunity for both to teach and to learn. If both pass this first test, the courtship develops into a professional marriage. In this *cultivation* phase, the mentor and protégé become a tiny learning organization in which understanding and knowledge peak to both their benefits. This intellectual gift-giving has something for everyone. The protégé gets invaluable knowledge that soon translates itself into talent, while the mentor receives a huge psychic gift—the loyalty and support of a junior colleague, the kind of give-back to the next generation that anyone over the age of forty regards as a form of immortality. It's all about passing on one's wisdom, almost an obligation when you've reached any level of success.

Ultimately, a successful mentor and protégé function as a single unit. This isn't easy. The impulse to hang back, to maintain the separatism of the mentor-protégé relationship in its early phases, is strong. In the critical moments of confrontation with the mill bosses, for instance, Norma Rae drags her feet, worrying about her insider's position in the mill, afraid of risk. But Reuben, knowing she's ready, shoves her directly into the line of fire with only the law to protect her. It is the force of his aggressive power plus her insider's authority that propel her back into the mill and create the powder keg needed to fuel the most persuasive act of their crusade: Norma Rae's silent, defiant stand, when she climbs up on a workbench in the center of the mill, her feet planted firmly, her UNION sign raised high above her head, as she waits to be dragged out by her bosses.

Her victory is signaled as the workers one by one begin to shut down their machines, joining Norma Rae in silent solidarity. Each machine that falls silent is a vote cast for the union. Together, Norma Rae and Reuben have gained a voice—and it's no coincidence that they speak loudest through this sudden, single act of silence. When the actual votes are finally in, weeks later, and tabulated to the cheers and chants of the millworkers—373 against the union, and 425 in favor—it is clear that this mentor and protégée have traveled an enormous distance together to achieve their goal.

## Building a Network of Mentors

So all this mentoring is indisputably well and good, but *Norma Rae* also perpetuates a very real and troublesome cultural stereotype that has become a near cliché: charismatic white male saves helpless white female. Where, one wonders, are the black female executives, for example, helping inexperienced white males grow as leaders? The limiting fact is, of course, that too few women—of any color—hold positions of power. Thus is the proverbial glass ceiling strengthened and preserved. What's a Norma Rae in search of a female mentor to do?

One solution, suggests *Wall Street Journal* writer Hal Lancaster, who recently reported on the problem, is to broaden the definition of mentoring. Why not, for example, think of mentoring not as a long-term helping relationship with one person, but instead as a series of short-term, small-dose "learning partners," each of whom is a female who specializes in particular skills? It's a continuous-learning "mentors for rent" program in which a female protégée might seek out a male mentor at one point but then need the advice of a female mentor at another time. "Or build a board of mentors," suggests Lancaster, "modeled after a corporate board of directors, an advisory panel of experts from inside and outside your organization."[5]

Still stymied? Network your way into a mentoring relationship through outfits like Women in Technology, a Sherman Oaks, California–based organization that has its members wear specially colored badges at its conferences so that protégée wannabes can spot them. It's also true that *Norma Rae*, in celebrating the benefits that can accrue to a positive and healthy mentoring relationship, tidily avoids its many hazards, as one of the few studies that investigates the taboo topic of mentoring failures points out.[6] One of the most frequently reported problems occurs in formalized mentoring programs that force "marriages" between mentor and protégé. It should come as no surprise that the risk of a mismatch is intolerably high. Then there's the tricky problem of the supervisor-as-mentor. It may seem efficient and effective—you know, "Let's make every manager a mentor"—but it's almost impossible for someone who has power over another's job assignments and performance appraisal to also be a trusted adviser.

Just imagine what might have happened if one of those good old boys down at the mill had been assigned to mentor Norma Rae. The ability to say "You're fired!" is an immediate and absolute disqualifier for mentorship. So is jealousy, the green-eyed monster that can quickly turn a mentoring relationship toxic. This paradoxical but very human tendency to regard others with envy can be triggered whenever the mentor discovers that the protégé has become a rising star in the organization. Under such conditions, the dark side of close personal relationships is revealed, and a once nurturing and supportive mentor can become a downright abusive enemy who stifles and suffocates a protégé's advancement.

It's important that mentors do not develop a dependency on their protégé who later becomes their assistant. When such protégés want to move on in the company, the senior manager may actually sabotage the move or delay it. The lesson in all this is that, as in all personal relationships, mentors can both help and hinder. Best to—as in marriage—become part of such a twosome with your eyes wide open.

Unlike successful marriages, however, robust mentor-protégé relationships come to an end. Researchers who study such processes have discovered that mentors and protégés usually part ways not because of any incompatibility, but just because of the inexorable geographical separation or job change. The relationship goes through a fundamental change in which both the mentor and the protégé grow remarkably, becoming peers and friends while at the same time trading dependence for independence.

Not surprisingly, this moment of transformation is captured dramatically in the final scene of *Norma Rae*:

REUBEN     So, what're you going to do now?

NORMA RAE     Live!

REUBEN     Yeh!

NORMA RAE     What else?

REUBEN        Well, you drop me a line once in a while,
              OK?

NORMA RAE     Anyone read your mail?

REUBEN        Well, my mother . . . How about I send you
              a copy of Dylan Thomas?

NORMA RAE     I already bought one for myself.

REUBEN        You did? Nobody can do anything for
              you, huh?

NORMA RAE     You've done something for me. A lot.

REUBEN        Well, you did something for us. A *mitzvah*.

NORMA RAE     What is that?

REUBEN        That's a good work. I don't say good-bye.
              I have been known to cry.

NORMA RAE     Well, what do you say?

REUBEN        Be happy. Be well.

NORMA RAE     Same to you.

REUBEN        [stammering] Best wishes don't seem hardly
              enough. I'd like to thank you. I do, I thank
              you for your companionship, your stamina,
              your horse sense, and a hundred and one
              laughs. I also enjoyed very much looking at
              your shining hair and your shining face.

NORMA RAE     Reuben, I think you like me.

REUBEN       I do.

NORMA RAE    I was going to buy you a tie clip or some
             shaving lotion or something, but I didn't
             know what you'd like.

REUBEN       Norma, what I've had from you has been
             sumptuous.

Clearly, their separation is painful as Reuben and Norma
Rae struggle to describe all that they have gained from one
another, and to say, simply, *thank you*. But when this mentor
and protégée separate, they will leave behind not two half-
formed leaders but two complete achievers—people who have
gained a new strength, will, and purpose all their own.

# PART THREE

## CONFLICTS AND TURNAROUNDS

*Eleven jurors in* 12 Angry Men *persuade the twelfth to change his vote to "not guilty."*

# SIX

# SOCRATIC LEADERSHIP

## *12 Angry Men*

### CAST OF CHARACTERS

Juror 1 *(Martin Balsam)*

Juror 2 *(John Fiedler)*

Juror 3 *(Lee J. Cobb)*

Juror 4 *(E. G. Marshall)*

Juror 5 *(Jack Klugman)*

Juror 6 *(Edward Binns)*

Juror 7 *(Jack Warden)*

Juror 8 *(Henry Fonda)*

Juror 9 *(Joseph Sweeney)*

Juror 10 *(Ed Begley)*

Juror 11 *(George Voskovec)*

Juror 12 *(Robert Webber)*

Director: Sidney Lumet

Screenwriter: Reginald Rose

You are not a Russian submarine commander hunching your way through treacherous, unknown waters; you are not an exploited mill-hand chafing under ignorant authoritarianism; you are not an astronaut launching your leadership values to the moon.

The 1957 film classic *12 Angry Men* does not require you to make any of the usual allegoric leaps that other films in this book have asked of you as they draw back their veils to reveal their values and lessons.

You are just an ordinary person, with your own set of values, heading downtown to meet with a bunch of other ordinary people with different values, to make a difficult decision in a hot, cramped room with uncomfortable chairs.

Sound familiar? We've all been in that room in one way or another, faced with agendas, attitudes, and values that are different from our own as we try to communicate and move an idea forward.

The courtroom drama, either fictive or real, compels as few other dramas can because it depends on a mental skill we frequently use, in even the most mundane situations—at dinner parties, at parent-teacher meetings, in boardrooms: the art of persuasion.

Persuasion—convincing strangers to consider new perspectives, new insights, new goals—is a fundamental, challenging task of leadership because it requires a deep investment of personal character, mental stamina, and a capacity for emotional insight perfectly balanced with the ability to reason. Logic and abundant feeling combine to persuade.

What's tricky about persuasion—and it's this point that *12 Angry Men* clarifies so thrillingly—is discerning the difference between getting others to think as you do, an obnoxious and risky use of power, and getting others to investigate themselves to discover common truths and facts—truths that transcend preference, prejudice, fear, and competitive jockeying. The courtroom drama, as a result, is usually a loud wake-up call as well, a reminder that there *are* such common truths.

All of these ideas certainly fuel the rich genre of legal movies, films that invariably take you on a journey into matters of race, gender, class, religion, society, and politics, insisting that a lone voice—if skilled in the art of persuasion—can lead others out of their limited views toward a common vision.

Think of Spencer Tracy portraying lawyer Henry Drummond (the character inspired by Clarence Darrow) in the film *Inherit the Wind* (1960) based on the real-life Scopes "Monkey Trial" of 1925. A high school science teacher is jailed for violating the precepts of the Bible by teaching Darwin's theories of evolution—banned by Tennessee state law—to his science class. His lawyer, hated by the townspeople, must—and does—persuade a jury that the Bible is "a good book. But it's not the only book."

Or consider Gregory Peck as Atticus Finch, the unswerving defense attorney in *To Kill a Mockingbird* (1962), who batters as best he can against the racial prejudice that is going to send an innocent black man to his death. In this film, prejudice overpowers persuasion—the proof is indisputable, and the jury ignores it in murderous defiance—reminding us of the potential power of the willful groupthink that can pervert a jury's objective process. These movie classics honor the highest truths of human justice.

But lately the process has been corrupted not so much by gullible jurors or by savvy lawyers' willfulness as by another, more insidious force: the consultants.

Jury *consultants*? No kidding. Increasingly, these $4,000-a-day juridical witch doctors have become powerful behind-the-scenes figures in the nation's courtrooms, particularly in high-profile cases. One of the most successful offers a toll-free hotline (1-800-A JURY DR) and hooks up videotaped witnesses and mock jurors to galvanic skin-response machines. The full dress rehearsals that follow are used to teach lawyer clients "pivotal point conditioning" so that they may, like courtroom *éminences grises*, predispose jurors to react in predictable ways. Another consultant reveals all we need to know about these legal hidden persuaders: "We help lawyers position their cases to juries in much the same way you would sell a bar of soap." Think Procter & Gamble meets Oliver Wendell Holmes.

Surveys, focus group interviews, psychological evaluations, two-way mirrors, experts armed with statistics—such gimmicks have made old lawyers' rules of thumb like *Jurors dressed in red acquit* and *Presbyterians are likely to convict* obsolete when it comes to picking and persuading a jury. But they have also increased the chance that this cornerstone of justice has become hopelessly flawed. Sadly, if you want to restore your faith in the jury system, you'd better watch a movie rather than visit a courtroom.

The best by far is *12 Angry Men*, unique among courtroom films because it's set after the trial is over, evidence has been presented, and witnesses have been heard. This film, in which the camera at times closes in so tightly on each juror's face that you can see every quiver, every blink of an eye, invites you to get inside each juror's psyche and watch the decision-making process as it slowly unfolds.

This is an old-fashioned movie—no quick cuts, no exhausting action, only meticulous observation of behavior—the perfect metaphor for an old style of justice, one in which marketing tricks and manipulation had no place. The film teaches a very practical leadership lesson. It is not enough to attempt to change the opinions and behavior of others: that is mere management. Only when others are influenced sufficiently to actually change has real leadership taken place.

The story of the film is based on the screenwriter's personal experience sitting on the jury of a manslaughter case in New York. The film stars Henry Fonda as an architect named Davis, but the stellar performances of the other eleven actors, including such luminaries as Lee J. Cobb, E. G. Marshall, and Ed Begley, turns *12 Angry Men* into a true ensemble tour de force.

The twelve jurors, known only by their numbers, are all white males. (This took place in 1957, when some state courts still barred women from jury service, and laws had yet to be passed requiring that all juries reflect the ethnic and racial mix of the communities they serve.) These twelve men have been instructed to decide, by unanimous agreement, the fate of a minority defendant, a boy accused of stabbing his father to death. A *guilty* verdict, and the boy will receive the death penalty. The movie begins as the jurors retire to separate fact from fancy, to deliberate the testimony of witnesses who claim to have seen and heard the murder, and to acquit if they have a reasonable doubt about the boy's guilt.

After some preliminaries in the steamy, claustrophobic jury room, the foreman calls for a vote. One by one, the jurors vote *guilty*, except for Juror 8 (Henry Fonda), who casts the only vote against conviction. Leadership of the group soon passes from the foreman to Juror 8, who proceeds to orchestrate, in ways that provide real insight into leadership by influence and persuasion, a complete reversal of the verdict.

Like Juror 8, the leader who persuades is not usually a flashy hero, or even necessarily someone who is able to stir affection, but is persistent and steady, a group navigator and reader of individual nuance. Such a leader is capable of slowing a decision down enough to highlight its flaws and virtues, and believes— whatever the outcome—in a careful, even lengthy process.

The persuader moves slowly, and often quietly. The persuader asks questions, explores variables, poses as others and supposes for others, following an unformed idea to its full realization. A persuader reads the room and shapes a text on the spot, inviting others to ask questions and to fill in the blanks through spirited dialogue and debate. It is only through the efforts of a persuader that an open-and-shut case or an ordinary meeting of a restless board of directors can become, as all effective meetings should, a meeting of minds. And the persuader is fascinated by minds—by the *meaning* of decisions, not just by their content or function—and delights in stirring others to think, reason, and build solid arguments. No wonder Juror 8 in

*12 Angry Men* is an architect, for a persuader designs what others will help to build, and leads the way without laying claim to the spotlight.

As the meeting of the jury begins, the mood is casual, good-natured, and brisk. Everyone seems convinced of the boy's guilt, impressed by the prosecuting attorney, and amused by the simplicity of their assigned task, which most of them hope to expedite quickly so they can get on with their day. Many of the men appear more burdened by the weather than by the weight of their responsibility. Juror 12 (Robert Webber), an advertising executive, actually feels lucky to be part of a murder trial, which he finds more entertaining than assault and burglary, and Juror 3 (Lee J. Cobb) expresses his disgust with a legal system that has ruined his day and cost him money.

## Raising Doubts

Only the one juror is quiet, and separates himself from the busy "let's get to it" mood that prevails. He will vote, alone against many, *not guilty*. How will he lead this emphatic, impatient group to, first, understand and respect his reasonable doubt, and then to explore it?

He has no specific arguments, no clear points to address—only a vague, nagging doubt about the decision the group wants to make and few explanations for that doubt. While he is certain that their decision is one that requires more time and seriousness, he is uncertain what to discuss.

This doubter must not only withstand the insults and disdain of the others, but must also challenge the common assumption that it is a majority's responsibility to change the loner. As one juror puts it, "It's up to the group of us to convince this gentleman that he's wrong, and we're right."

Juror 8, though, is willing to trust his doubt, to voice it, and to stop the seemingly efficient process that is under way. He challenges no one directly, but requests a slow down to discuss the issues. Meanwhile, the harried jury foreman, who exudes the naive enthusiasm of someone who has just been trained in efficient meeting techniques, tries to speed things up. "We have all this work to do," he implores, "there's no point in staying here all night." Then he pleads, "Hey, let's hold it down. These side arguments are only holding us up!"

Then there's the patronizing putdown directed at Juror 8, "Let us know what you're thinking, and, uh, we might be able to show you where you're mixed up." And finally, the silencing: "Let's stop the arguing, we're only wasting time." This group's nominal leader is obviously focused on urgency, the imperative of speed. "OK, fellows, let's take our seats. OK, now, let's get down to business. Who wants to start it off? Go!"

Next time your 1:00 meeting takes on a life of its own, and at 4:30 only two of seven agenda points have been covered, understand this kind of pressure. All that checking of watches, tapping of pencils, stifled yawning, and squirming you see is the unmistakable sign that you've lost 'em. It happens. After all, we've been inured to a sense of urgency that leads us to treat crowded daily agendas as if they were the stuff of true leadership—the more meetings on the calendar, the more power we possess. Speed is everything, and especially so in meetings.

No wonder research has shown that most meetings occur in hallways as harried managers bolt through their day. And on those rare occasions when they do sit down in some conference room, God help anyone who yells, "Hold it, we've gotta think this through some more." You can almost hear the other members of the group sigh in unison, "We don't have time for this."

They don't realize what Juror 8 knows: that quality decisions require passionate discussion, debate, and even argument. And that takes time. Ironically, it is this "dragging on," this prolonging of the meeting in that jury room in *12 Angry Men*, that prevents a rush to judgment and makes the right verdict possible. But you would be hard-pressed to find this strategy mentioned in a how-to book on effective meeting protocol. There's everything else, of course—advice to "be on time," to "gauge your contribution based on where the group is in the decision-making process," to "do your homework," even to "choose your seat carefully so as not to offend some panjandrum." But you won't find one page on the important art of intentionally decelerating a meeting.

Let's consider one approach Juror 8 uses to put the brakes on the lightning-fast jury deliberations in *12 Angry Men*. He knows that speed kills when it comes to running a meeting in which discovering the truth is the goal.

JUROR 10     Boy oh boy! There's always one.

JUROR 7     Well, whadda we do now?

JUROR 8     I guess we talk.

JUROR 10    You really think he's innocent?

JUROR 8     I don't know.

JUROR 3     Well, you sat in court with the rest of us. You
            heard what we did. The kid's a dangerous killer.
            You could see it.

JUROR 8     He's eighteen years old.

JUROR 3     Well, that's old enough. He stabbed his own
            father four inches into the chest. They proved it
            a dozen different ways in court. Would you like
            me to list them for you?

JUROR 8     No.

JUROR 10    Then what do you want?

JUROR 8     I just want to talk.

For much of this meeting, Juror 8 offers no specific arguments or points, but he nonetheless gets everyone to empathize, question, and role-play. He wants to embark on an intellectual quest, and he enthusiastically invites others to join him.

## Bad Reasoning Put to Good Use

Some critics have said that Juror 8's approach is, at first, thoroughly unscientific and even illogical, arguing as he does from ignorance. As Brooklyn College's Jonathan Adler has accurately noted, Fonda's character in the first third of *12 Angry Men* "repeatedly appeals to mere suppositions and possibilities, typically without the least attempt, as he often admits, to back them up as at all probable."[1] Perhaps, though, as Adler has put it, "If good reasoning can be put to ill use, bad reasoning can be put to good."

Juror 8 begins this process by simply imagining himself as the boy on trial. In fact, he has even done a little additional research for the meeting by strolling through the boy's neighborhood. He has followed not logic but a hunch, and he has found a knife just like the supposedly unique murder weapon. Thus armed with nothing but doubt and a single visual aid that implies alternative theories, he persists.

Juror 8's steady reiteration of doubt, backed by one literal point of persuasion, gives this loner the opportunity to evaluate the attitudes, motives, prejudices, and values of the others around him. He must read the others' responses to his doubt and discern whether he has gained any footing at all in his quest for a more thorough investigation of the case.

He's got to be a great listener. He hears the bigotry of Juror 10 (Ed Begley), who rants against minorities ("They're born liars!"); he hears the subtle allegiance that forms between certain jurors who share backgrounds and experiences; he hears Juror 3's paternal rage; he hears an old man's brief defense of the loner's position ("It's only one night. A boy may die."); and he hears several collisions of value. Acting on what he hears, he gambles his position, trusting that at least one will vote with him:

JUROR 8    I have a proposition to make to all of you. I'm
           gonna call for another vote. I want you eleven

men to vote by secret written ballot. I'll abstain.
If there are eleven votes for guilty, I won't stand
alone, we'll take in the guilty verdict to the judge
right now. But if anyone votes not guilty, we stay
here and talk it out.

This juror has just enough confidence to propose his own
procedure, and to effect a change.

Believe it or not, *12 Angry Men*, a film that depends so heavily upon the protagonist's ability to read, and then act on, other
persons' behaviors, has itself become a device for measuring
this capacity in future leaders. Researchers, wanting to confirm
studies suggesting that there might be a link between such
social acuity and the capacity to lead, administered a test to 117
college students that measured their *cognitive complexity*, or ability to read the behavioral clues of others. People with high cognitive complexity scores tend to be more empathetic and
people-oriented and make better leaders.[2]

The students then watched the first 38 minutes of *12 Angry
Men*, up to the point at which the jurors are about to take their
second vote. Then they were given a form depicting the jury
seating arrangement and a description of each juror and asked
to predict the order in which the jurors would change their
votes from *guilty* to *not guilty*. Not surprisingly, the students
with higher cognitive complexity scores were also better
predictors of the behavior of the jurors in *12 Angry Men*. The
lesson from all this is that the ability to read other people and
situations accurately is an important correlate to effective
leadership.

## The Value of Shared Values

When one juror changes his vote to *not guilty*, it's not because he has agreed with Juror 8's arguments. It is because he recognizes that they share certain values. "He gambled for support," he says, "and I gave it to him. I respect his motives."

With the support of one other—it's great to have a partner to launch a persuasive campaign—Juror 8 gains energy to further his quest. He continues to shift roles, trying to see from the perspectives of all the people involved—the lawyers, each witness—and to ask his fellow jurors a multitude of questions that require all of the group members to reflect on their own knowledge, experience, backgrounds, logic, and imagination.

He is a master of inquiry, rarely imposing his own conclusions on the group but enthusiastically, energetically encouraging others to get involved with ideas, discrepancies, and alternative scenarios that convey his respect for their capacities to think.

Sometimes Juror 8 knows the answers to his own questions. On other occasions he asks questions to which he has no answers himself. He admits ignorance. "I don't really know what the truth is," he says, and concedes later, "I don't know, I'm guessing."

By asking a wide range of questions to which he may or may not know the answers, frequently feigning ignorance, Juror 8 is exercising a kind of leadership that is counterintuitive to most of us, who likely have been taught quite the reverse—that leadership is about omniscient certainty. It is, rather, almost always about uncertainty. It is more than trained reactions and quick responses; it is not a science with tried-and-true techniques. It cannot be reduced to a list of how-tos. And, since it seeks truth, it is philosophic in nature.

Leaders very often *are* philosophers, exploring the purpose, meaning, and execution of ideas as action. Suitably, Juror 8 uses the Socratic method of leadership, which is founded on the Greek philosopher Socrates' belief that answers to questions can only be achieved through active inquiry that allows others to arrive at their own answers. Socrates thought that questions of ethics and virtue—the sort that should drive a justice system—could only be answered with every questioner relying upon self-knowledge and self-examination.

This approach to the leadership task also has at its essence a kind of genuine humility rarely found among leaders, articulated by Socrates in *Apology* when he says, "I know very well that I am not wise, even in the smallest degree." Combined with Socrates's more famous aphorism that "an unexamined life is not worth living," the implication is clear. Leaders, more than anyone else, can help themselves by being open to criticism. Like Juror 8, they can only achieve this if their leadership is rooted—as Leonard Grob has pointed out—"in that exercise of humility which is the mark of the philosopher."[3]

Juror 8 uses the Socratic method, some good math, and a sense of spatial relations to stir the eleven others to an exciting discussion about some complicated evidence, and provokes a radical shift of perspective. Perhaps you remember those brain teasers that plagued you during your school days. Something like "Two trains leave their stations 20 miles apart at 8:00 A.M.

One is traveling 10 miles per hour, the other 15 miles per hour. At what time will the two trains meet?" Juror 8 shows his capacity for solving such puzzlers brilliantly. After a great deal of discussion, he sums up their realizations:

JUROR 8   Let's take two pieces of testimony and try to put them together. First, the old man in the apartment downstairs. He says he heard the boy say, "I'm gonna kill you!" and a split-second later heard a body hit the floor. One second later, right? Second, the woman across the street swore positively she looked out of the window and saw the killing through the last two cars of a passing elevated train, right? The last two cars of the train. We've agreed that it takes 10 seconds for a train to pass a given point. Since the woman saw the killing through the last two cars, we can assume that the body hit the floor just as the train went by. Therefore, the train had been roaring by the old man's window a full 10 seconds before the body hit the floor. The old man—according to his own testimony—"I'm gonna kill you!"; body hitting the floor a split-second later—would have had to hear the boy make this statement with the El roaring past his nose. It's not possible he could have heard it!

In leadership, it helps to have remarkable powers of deduction.

## Igniting Others

After this, the room starts jumping with mental fire and all the seismic energy of an idea rumbling to the surface. And a physical transformation begins as well, as men lean forward, leap to their feet, circle one another with a focused knowledge that there's news on the table that must be dealt with.

This is no longer a routine, low-energy meeting, a mere gathering of the mindless herd. This meeting has become for every man a crucible of character and judgment. Regardless of what they decide, their decision can no longer be made in a mood of complacency.

The discourse moves from monologue (the language of bureaucrats and tyrants) to dialogue (the language of equality) to multilogue (the language of engagement). In this third stage, the conversation suggests that things have gotten out of control, as if each point were a billiard ball caroming off another as the jurors react energetically to each other. The search for truth, it seems, is invariably a noisy enterprise, and sometimes—as we learn in this movie—an angry one.

The diversity in background, ideas, and experiences of the jurors makes this a group in which conflict is assured. Juror 8 first provokes it, then harnesses it, then uses it.

Too bad most people shy away from the roiling disagreement that is so well dramatized in *12 Angry Men*. Of course meetings should not become shouting matches, but they should have nearly unbridled energy. One way to achieve this is to use, not resolve, conflict. That's what happened at Boehringer Ingelheim, the global pharmaceutical company, when a team of organizational development specialists from the company's offices in Canada, the United States, and Mexico was formed. Conflict, according to Michael Leonetti, director of organization effectiveness, started immediately. Within six months, the tension among team members was so great that they had become, quite literally, angry men.

Wisely, they did not attempt to suppress this anger, because they knew that energetic disagreement is a healthy part of the collaborative process. Instead of shying away from the conflict, they wrestled with it head-on until they eventually reached consensus on the best corporate-wide learning strategy. "The process didn't always feel good," Leonetti told a reporter, "but it did work."[4]

## Avoiding Groupthink

Such agreeing to disagree is a sure antidote for groupthink, that tendency for groups to gravitate mindlessly toward collective miscalculations that can do great harm. True, we consign really important decisions to groups instead of individuals on the assumption that, as in investing, spreading our eggs around in several baskets makes good sense. But too often, the results these teams, task forces, committees, panels, and powwows achieve lend credence to Nietzsche's observation that madness is the exception in individuals but the rule in groups.

Conformity pressure, it seems, reliably causes persons in groups to drive for consensus at any cost, as Irving Janis has pointed out in *Victims of Groupthink*, a remarkable book in which the author persuasively asserts that the Bay of Pigs invasion, the decision to escalate the Korean War, and other debacles were the result of independent critical thinking being replaced by groupthink. He might well have been describing eleven of the *12 Angry Men.*

Juror 8's role at the point of engagement and conflict diminishes as he steps back to allow others to seize the subject matter. He contributes questions and ideas when he's needed—he is, after all, a stimulator, and when the other jurors reach a conversational impasse, he's right there with more ideas and questions to launch them again into the subject. He also demands some very specific calculations and reenactments to verify their conclusions, making sure their ideas are backed by the facts. He's not interested in discovery without validity or in transformation without purpose.

There's a lot more going on here than a simple discovery of facts and recognition of a flawed reasoning that was initially leading this group astray. Certainly Juror 8 has refused to be led by appearances and generalizations. Instead, he insists on being led by his intelligence, his convictions, and by his effective communication with others. But it is what he requires of those others in the process that really ignites change.

1. Each man is invited to use a wide variety of skills introduced by Juror 8. Notice how the other jurors begin to question, role-play, and empathize, too.

2. They must all reflect on their own backgrounds and experience, contributing their unique perspectives to the process. Juror 5 (Jack Klugman), raised in a slum, reflects

on all that he learned growing up in a violent neighborhood to reveal key information about the angle of the
knife; Juror 9 (Joseph Sweeney) reflects on his experience as an old man to reveal the possible motive of a
false witness; Juror 4 (E. G. Marshall) must consider his
own handicap—weak eyesight—to acknowledge the
weakness of a questionable eyewitness.

3. Each juror must acknowledge his own values and priorities—in short, his character—to discover the truth.

Until they discover those truths, they will be ineffective
decision makers. Juror 8 gives his colleagues an opportunity to
become engaged—and enraged—with each other, revealing
themselves, challenging a too-easy consensus, forging a pathway
to the truth. They may be evaluating evidence and disputing
their understanding of it, but far more important, they are discovering themselves and their motives.

What to do, then, with Juror 3, the angry father, and Juror
10, the bigot, whose capacity to think and discover is crippled
by prejudice? "Prejudice always obscures the truth," Juror 8
counsels, knowing that these people cannot be persuaded in
the usual ways because they long ago surrendered their interest
in logic. Prejudice is obviously wedded to stasis and power, and
is usually governed by emotional imperatives that eclipse
appeals to reason. Juror 10 is silenced not by logic but by the
humiliation of a reprimand from another juror; and Juror 3,
clearly ill-equipped to think and speak effectively, is silenced
only after this direct and unexpected confrontation:

Juror 3    [We're] letting him slip through our fingers!

Juror 8    Slip through our fingers? Are you his executioner?

Juror 3    I'm one of 'em.

Juror 8    Perhaps you'd like to pull the switch.

Juror 3    For this kid, you bet I would.

Juror 8    I feel sorry for you. What it must feel like, to
           want to pull the switch! Ever since you walked
           into this room, you've been acting like a self-
           appointed public avenger! You want to see this
           boy die because you personally want it! Not
           because of the facts. You're a sadist!

Such direct, well-targeted verbal assaults are a necessity even
for the quiet persuader, who must confront the irrationality of
others—the loudmouths, the ones who often have a lot of
power. What breaks Juror 3's stance is his own final recognition
of himself. Destroyer, Abuser, Avenger. He sees the truth and
relents. He has not only served justice, but has also learned that
the source of his wrath is not the young defendant but his own
son. His catharsis has taken place.


## A Model Meeting

How could a meeting be more efficient or more effective?
*12 Angry Men* gives us a remarkable view of unremarkable people in a remarkable discussion, an inside look at ordinary people put into an exceptional situation. As Jay Boyer puts it in his

profile of *12 Angry Men*'s director, "[the camera] follows one jury member, and picks up another when a second character crosses his path. A group is being formed before our eyes, and within that group, relationships are being established."[5] The film reminds us that imagination, reason, verbal skill, and a love and respect for capacities of the mind can stir a creative energy that will accomplish more than just a decision. The leader who persuades doesn't aim for just agreement, but for a recognition of the lineaments of character—the very hearts of the people he works with, whatever those hearts contain.

*12 Angry Men*, without gimmicks or pretense, shot in one tiny room, chronicling a few hours in the lives of twelve rather everyday human beings, teaches much about leadership. And not one consultant was used. The tribute to the jury system given by Juror 11 seems to ring true:

> JUROR 11   This, I have always thought, is a remarkable thing about democracy, that we are—what is the word?—notified! That we are notified by mail to come down to this place—to decide on the guilt or innocence of a man we have never heard of before. We have nothing to gain or lose by our verdict. This is one of the reasons why we are strong.

Not every decision, of course, is a life-and-death decision like this one. But *12 Angry Men* cracks open old assumptions, showing us that a quiet person can lead, majorities don't always rule, slowing down can be more useful than speeding up, decisions cannot and should not succeed independent of their meaning, and we are responsible every day for the moves we make.

*General Frank Savage's (Gregory Peck) hard-nosed speech gives his troops the shock treatment in* Twelve O'Clock High.

# SEVEN

# Turning Around a Troubled Organization

## *Twelve O'Clock High*

### Cast of Characters

General Frank Savage *(Gregory Peck)*

Colonel Keith Davenport *(Gary Merrill)*

Major Harvey Stovall *(Dean Jagger)*

General Pritchard *(Millard Mitchell)*

Lieutenant Colonel Ben Gately *(Hugh Marlowe)*

Director: Henry King

Screenwriters: Sy Bartlett and Beirne Lay, Jr.

War, with its strategies, opposing forces, rules of engagement, high stakes, and zero-sum orientation in which a victor's gain is an opponent's loss, has gained unsettling power of late as a metaphor for business. Stroll the aisle of any bookstore's business section and you'll find scores of texts jampacked with warrior tactics.

Of course the lessons of Sun Tzu's extraordinary work *The Art of War*, or a study of history's great military leaders, from Alexander the Great to Norman Schwarzkopf, can provide perspectives and attitudes useful, often essential, to the successful business life. But it would do us all well to remember that although for many unfortunate souls war is indeed a business, business is not—in even its most extreme cases of cutthroat offense or tragic failure—war. To begin to equate the two, without drawing what would seem to be the obvious boundaries, is to forfeit your balance and sense of perspective as a leader, to borrow from the crises of the world to romanticize or legitimize your work.

While war stories, true and fictive, are undeniably valuable sources for leadership study (extremity, of course, puts successful and unsuccessful strategies into sharp relief), they can also invite a too-simple blurring of the lines between business and battle.

## Metaphorical Dangers

Be warned: metaphors are powerful. They are the prisms through which we interpret the world. They can shape our beliefs and trigger our behavior. But they are also incomplete, only partially accurate portrayals of objective realities.

So the first and best favor you can do for yourself before studying a war film as leadership text is to determine clearly what distinguishes the business leader from the squadron leader, what separates a high-stakes deal from an airborne dogfight, what defines a life-destroying failure of management, and what defines a lost war.

If you have trouble discerning these boundaries in your own mind, you're in no shape to go to the office. Chances are, your employees fear you, and your tactics are fueled only by blind ambition. Anyone who suggests to you that war's leadership tactics are fail-safe in the office is leading you astray, or has, through a mistaken enthusiasm, taken the metaphor too far. Here's a tip: when you hear the catchphrases of movies become catchall ideas for work, listen carefully. The trendy command from the 1996 film *Jerry Maguire*—"Show me the money!"—is not to be confused literally or theoretically with Captain John Miller's whispered plea to a surviving soldier in the final carnage of Steven Spielberg's 1998 film *Saving Private Ryan*—"Earn this." The language of imperative appears to be the same; the stakes most certainly do not.

At its best, a war film can guide us through the horrors and triumphs of warfare without allowing us the luxury of a self-indulgent or blindly self-serving viewing. Courageous, valiant, and refreshingly unequivocal films like *Bataan* (1943), *Guadalcanal Diary* (1949), *Sands of Iwo Jima* (1949), and *Beach Red* (1967) come quickly to mind, as does *Twelve O'Clock High* (1949), a movie whose opening credits announce that its aim is not to glamorize warfare with Hollywood charm, despite the charm of its leading actors, but to honor and recall with respect the battles of the daylight precision bombers of World War II.

These actual battles are woven into the story elements of this film, never letting us forget the realities of courage and death that put war movies in their proper place as elegiac efforts. Such restraint, and its unerring focus on a single B-17 bomber group and the two very different leaders who commanded it, may explain why it won several Academy Awards in its day and has, ever since, been a mainstay in leadership training both private and public.

The training industry hype for *Twelve O'Clock High* has been as expected. "Immerse yourself," reads a typical brochure, "in an advanced case study of 'Situational Leadership' in action with the classic, award-winning film *Twelve O'Clock High*. The movie soon becomes a grim metaphor for our industry," it spiels on, "and a dramatic and poignant reminder of the knowledge, experience, skill, motivation, commitment, sacrifice, flexibility, humor, and leadership that's necessary to succeed in a business besieged by potentially deadly competitive forces."[1]

Even the Harvard Business School has gotten into the act, adding its lofty imprimatur to the film by publishing an "Orientation for Viewing *Twelve O'Clock High*" that includes not only an organization chart for the 918th Bomber Group but also provides what it calls "space for student note taking on various stages in the process of organizational change." Watch this film, Harvard's catalog cheerfully promises, and you will learn much about the

- management of change,
- management styles,
- managerial behavior,
- managerial skills,

- organizational behavior,
- organizational change, and
- organizational management.[2]

Our take on *Twelve O'Clock High* is different. Sure, it teaches much about leadership style and turning around a troubled organization. But we think it also serves as an unforgettable cautionary tale about the costs of demanding maximum effort from yourself and others.

## Trying to Define Maximum Effort

In *Twelve O'Clock High*, everyone seems to be trying to define something called *maximum effort*. But what *is* maximum effort? Most of us assume we're just to give our all—to push past our supposed limits and succeed, like Jim Lovell in *Apollo 13*. Surely that's the hope of all those wishing to lead well in any situation. But the problems that Colonel Keith Davenport (Gary Merrill) and General Frank Savage (Gregory Peck), the film's two protagonists, encounter pursuing maximum effort will take you deep into some challenging leadership terrain: balancing the so-called "hard" leadership issues of performance, discipline, and group cohesiveness with the "softer" issues of empathy, loyalty, and open compassion. And on this journey, you may discover a confusing but essential paradox: in leadership, the soft stuff is very often the hard stuff.

The story of *Twelve O'Clock High* is a memory—specifically, the memory of Major Harvey Stovall (Dean Jagger), an aging former member of the 918th Bomber Group. In the opening scene of the film, he buys a cheap mug that has, for him, all the value of experience in the company of two remarkable leaders. This first dreamlike sequence in which Stovall makes a nostalgic return visit to his dilapidated World War II air base suddenly plunges you—thanks to a smoothly executed series of flashbacks—into the midst of the strategic bombing campaign against the German Third Reich. You will witness the missions, circumstances, and attempts of men trying to determine, in the midst of a lot of dying, the meaning of maximum effort—or, what does it *mean* to give your all?

Everyone, it seems, in the 918th wants to know the answer, which seems to have something to do with juggling group tasks and individual psychologies simultaneously, though no one has a clue how to do that. The group's doctor is at a loss. *Maximum effort* could mean the physical or psychological limits of performance. Equally baffled is the group's leader, Keith Davenport, who wants to know how hard to drive his team. General Pritchard (Millard Mitchell), who issues the orders for the 918th's missions, has no better idea than those he sends into battle, though he insists that his leaders deliver what he can't define and prefers that his group leaders avoid questions of individual motive and act without diagnosing themselves or their men. He'll send Frank Savage in to lead the 918th in the hope that Savage will figure *maximum effort* out, inspire his men, and succeed without crumbling as his failed predecessor Davenport has done.

At first, it's pretty hard to believe things could have gone wrong for Keith Davenport, who is a kind of rumpled father figure to his "boys," revered by everyone. He dutifully practices the kind of participative, open leadership espoused by social scientists, whose predilection for democratic leadership, subordinate participation, and freedom of action have come to be expected in a constitutional society. Davenport is everywhere in the opening scenes of *Twelve O'Clock High*: helping to pull the wounded out of a burning B-17, rushing off to the briefing room to protect his pilots from the quietly methodical inquiries of their interrogators, mothering shell-shocked 18-year-olds who fear (often rightly) they may not be made of the right stuff, grumbling to headquarters that the order requiring his pilots to drop their bombs at a dangerously low 9,000 feet is suicidal insanity.

But it is Davenport's attitudes and leadership beliefs that will clarify and define the very opposite terms of leadership his replacement, Frank Savage, pursues. Why? We start to discern the answer in this scene between Davenport and the company doctor, where Davenport shows not only the strain of leading his shaky group into daily hazardous missions but his utter confusion over his group's increasing sense of fear and failure and his inability to define *maximum effort*:

|  |  |
|---|---|
| Doc | That's getting to be your diet, isn't it? [Coffee] and cigarettes? . . . |
| Colonel Davenport | Thanks for worrying about me, Doc. Only don't. What about the rest of 'em? |
| Doc | That brings us to the two answers. On that list of twenty-eight men asking to be excused from tomorrow's mission, three times more than normal, they give a lot of reasons. Colds, mostly. And most of them haven't got colds. And that doesn't mean that they've |

suddenly gone yellow. It just means they're
getting their bellies full. Now do I okay them
physically and mark 'em duty? How much
can a man take? What's physical and what
isn't?

COLONEL      Well, the rules say a man ought to go right
DAVENPORT    up to the point where he may endanger his
             crew. I wish I knew what that meant. If I
             did, I'd tell you.

DOC          Well, can you tell me this: do I okay Bishop
             for tomorrow?

COLONEL      He had a tough deal. Jesse's a tough boy.
DAVENPORT

DOC          How tough? What happened today must've
             done something to him inside. It had to cost
             him something. Somebody's got to give me a
             policy. Some kind of yardstick. I wish you'd
             tell me what a *maximum effort* means!

COLONEL      Doc, I wish I knew. I wish I could answer
DAVENPORT    that one.

A lot of wishing going on here, and few answers. Everyone
in the 918th—and, one assumes, elsewhere—seems in need of
a clear policy, someone to outline the limits. Put simply, the
918th is badly in need of leadership. But in many ways Daven-
pot has already chosen to draw his own limits: he will not
sacrifice individuals for group integrity; he will absorb all indi-

vidual errors as his own; he will carry the burden of his men's limitations and stand between them and the difficulty of their necessary tasks. He is, in short, reinforcing private fear and suffering instead of leading his men beyond their doubts. His men feel fear, exhaustion, and frustration twofold because they see their condition reflected and affirmed by their leader. Davenport is empathetic to the point of collapse—his own, as well as his group's.

## A Nice Guy as Leader

Keith Davenport's hypersensitivity to his men's struggles has rendered him nearly useless to the task before him: to carry out a dangerous mission and achieve a larger goal. While nobody argues against the absolute decency of Davenport—including all his superiors, who worry over his performance and try to steer him back toward group priorities—they all recognize that Davenport's basic control of his own emotions has dwindled considerably. This is one way that "sensitive" leaders can lose authority, purpose, and, in the eyes of most leadership pundits, legitimacy. Davenport is so busy "feeling his men's pain" that he has ceased to move forward. While there's no question that Keith Davenport is a caring friend, a shoulder to lean on, he has lost his loyalty to the goal of his squadron, and resists his assignments.

Inevitably, Davenport's worry for his crews robs each crew member of a personal sense of responsibility and priority. And in a pivotal leader debriefing, Davenport exposes his soft leadership stance by trying to take the bullets for his men's mistakes, as we see in the following scene in which Zimmerman, one of the group's navigators, admits to General Pritchard a critical, and deadly, mistake:

| | |
|---|---|
| GENERAL PRITCHARD | Maybe the mistake lay in not going on to the secondary target once you were late. |
| COLONEL DAVENPORT | But I figured we could make up the time, catch up with the other groups. We could have, too, if it hadn't been for our stinking luck. |
| GENERAL PRITCHARD | Luck? What luck was that? |
| ZIMMERMAN | It wasn't luck, sir. It was my fault. |
| COLONEL DAVENPORT | It wasn't anybody's fault. |
| GENERAL PRITCHARD | I'd like to hear the lieutenant's version. |
| ZIMMERMAN | Yes, sir. We had to alter the navigation in flight, sir, to cross the enemy coast here. We picked up an error, a wind change, and I missed the checkpoint here at Saint-Lô. By the time I caught it here, at Rheims, it had cost us three minutes. We never made it up. |
| COLONEL DAVENPORT | If there's any fault, it's mine, sir. I was in command. I ordered the change in flight plan. The weather was thick enough. It could have happened to anyone. |

No wonder this thoroughly nice guy has become so ineffectual. He blames bad luck and eschews accountability. As a
result, he has unwittingly transformed his troops into airborne
couch potatoes, flyers who have lost their edge, who stray slop-
pily from formation and all too regularly drop their bombs—
if they drop them at all—in the wrong places. The 918th is a
parody of its purpose, which is to destroy the enemy's capacity
to support surface forces and its will to continue the war.
Instead, under Davenport's bumbling leadership, the 918th has
become the gang that couldn't shoot straight, an almost welcome sight to the Luftwaffe pilots who so efficiently and sys-
tematically blast its bombers out of the air.

Clearly it's time for another leader. And when Davenport
announces belligerently, "General, I don't believe in chopping
off heads because of one mistake. Well, I just don't think that's
any way to run a group," the general fires him.

## A Savage Arrives

General Frank Savage thinks Davenport was off the mark with
his "sensitive" leadership, and he tackles the same group with
exactly the opposite approach. Call him a callous martinet if
you will, but—like it or not—he looks like a leader, sounds
like a leader, and acts like a leader. Savage, you suspect, may just
be the right person to take on the difficult task of trying to
turn the 918th into a winner again.

You know it from the moment his staff car pauses for a few
minutes before entering the 918th's air base. In a scene proving
once again that in leadership, as in the theater, entrances are
everything, Savage stands comfortably alongside the car as it

idles just outside the gate. He reaches in to offer his driver a cigarette, then amiably lights it for him. You expect banter. Yet, after a few puffs, he stares off into the distance as if to get into his role, then flings the cigarette down, crushing it with his heel. You get bluster, and a dramatic metamorphosis. "All right, Sergeant," snarls Savage, as if ordering a full brigade to attention. He is so good at simultaneously playing both good cop *and* bad cop, you just know that everyone and everything on that base is about to be challenged.

Some might think this ability to transform oneself from good guy to bad guy on demand smacks of hypocrisy. Yet such role-playing—the capacity to consciously *choose* a leadership style befitting the moment—is anything but disingenuous acting. Steeling oneself is, in fact, a critical leadership moment of truth. And just as an actor about to take the stage may seek a private moment of reflection before "going on," so too must a leader consciously prepare to assume what John Keegan has so aptly called the "mask of command."[3] Seizing the moment, it seems, may call for considerable thespian ability.

What's more, such tyrannical behavior may, on occasion, be called for. Consider, for example, the case of Kay R. Whitmore, former chairman and CEO of Eastman Kodak, who was fired by Kodak's board for the very simple reason that he was, to use Savage's comment describing Keith Davenport, "a first-rate guy."

Whitmore's participative and permissive leadership style, it seems, made it impossible for him to make the tough decisions (laying off thousands of employees, slashing research budgets, and selling underperforming divisions) that were required to turn the troubled Kodak around. Robert Stemple, too, was removed by the General Motors board because he was unwilling to make the unpopular call to close unproductive plants and to take on the giant automaker's formidable unions. Then there's John "Jack the Ripper" Grundhofer, who was brought in by Minneapolis-based First Bank System to turn things around. "I'll do whatever I have to do, however draconian," announced Grundhofer. "You have to manage tough to survive." Extraordinary times, apparently, call for extraordinary, even tyrannical, leaders.[4]

Mastering a repertoire of leadership roles, and then choosing which one to play, and at what time, is of course the *sine qua non* of the exceptional leader. And such theatrical flexibility is invaluable in the kind of organizational turnaround that Savage is trying to achieve. It may fly in the face of a growing number of New Wave absolutist leadership experts who, with their own special kind of tyranny, peddle the latest universal value system for all mankind, boiled down to a list of seven immutable steps, five keys, or four habits. But solid leadership theory reveals what no self-help quackery can: leaders play roles.

Which ones? The answer can be arrived at only by using the frustratingly elusive calculus of leadership, which, boiled down to its essence, is: it depends. On the circumstances. On the leader's personality. On the followers' capabilities. The point, of course, is that when it comes to leading, there is rarely one best way. Like it or not, no tidy prescription or orderly to-do list of traits or behaviors can take the place of common sense and the ability to read the situation.

And when it comes to taking the measure of things, Savage is a quick study. In hours, he's concluded that the 918th has come to overvalue individual freedoms over what is good for the group, has lost confidence in itself, and needs to rekindle its pride. And he knows that if you don't change the culture in an outfit that is in serious difficulty, you're not going to turn it around.

## Shaking Up the Troops

What is Savage's agenda? He'll break every personal alliance he sees among the men, redirecting their attention to the mission; he'll demand that every man take responsibility for his own errors; he'll shame men who fail to do their job; and he'll refuse, for some time, to see any man as special. His mission? He'll give back pride as he challenges every man to lead himself toward personal success for the good of the group.

Unlike Davenport, Savage excuses nothing, not even an opened collar, a failure to salute, or a wordy answer to a "yes or no" question. He'll foist his own strength of will onto the group, demanding that they see him as an officer, not as a friendly face.

Such reality-checking gives Savage a distinct advantage over the permanently laid-back Keith Davenport. Here is a leader who is anything but a wimp, one who won't sit on the sidelines waiting for someone else to make the gut-wrenching decisions that are necessary to turn around an ailing organization. Savage alone seems to possess the ability to succeed, even though he has limited resources (there aren't enough airplanes) and a sense of urgency (those factories must be destroyed soon). He is able to deliver, better than anyone else, a sense of mission.

Savage knows that for now, he must assume the role of tyrant. They wanted policies? They've got 'em now, and there'll be no room for sweeping displays of emotion or confusion.

The worst offenders receive his swift discipline. He's studied all his men, and he responds to each of them with absolute
precision, keeping assignments and objectives as his primary
targets and rarely missing his mark. Maximum effort, as far as
Savage is concerned, pushes past fear, past history, past self, and
into responsibility and risk. He expects no less from his men,
and—honorably—no less from himself.

This kind of shake-up doesn't go over well, especially in a
floundering organization. But ultimately it's a necessity. Jan
Muczyk and Robert Steel have studied the effect of leadership
style on successful turnarounds, and have concluded that Sav-
age-like control may well be called for when, as in the 918th
Bomber Group, the organization is *in extremis*. This is true,
they point out, even though democratic leadership and respect
for individual autonomy is very much the cultural norm in U.S.
society, a kind of ethical necessity for everyone who embraces
its basic beliefs.[5] "We often lose sight of the fact," they write,
"that the directive autocrat is not some misanthrope or ogre, but
merely a person who is paid to make the important decisions,
set the salient goals, and direct subordinates along the way—
especially in a crisis when subordinates tend to rally around a
decisive leader." Their research has led them to conclude what
General Savage seems to know intuitively: that Davenport's
nice-guy democratic leadership simply doesn't work in this situation. It's time for a more no-nonsense approach to leading
the 918th.

Davenport, not surprisingly, disagreed with the order
requiring the 918th to begin the dangerous low-level bombing
needed to inflict real damage to Germany's submarine pens.
He had even committed the unpardonable sin of criticizing it

in front of his men. Savage, on the other hand, not only embraces the strategy of daylight precision bombing, but is able to communicate its importance to the group's pilots. And he unwaveringly harps on a core value that has as much to do with carrying out the mission as it does with morale. "This group, this group, this group," he drills in. "That has to be your loyalty, your only reason for being. . . ." This litany is meant to teach the all-important lesson that a b-17 group's defensive integrity is entirely dependent upon the tightness of its formation; any pilot who drops out to help a buddy puts the whole enterprise at risk.

Orit Gadiesh, ceo of Bain & Company, the blue-ribbon consulting firm, refers to this capacity to give direction to an organization as "finding and following true north." Gadiesh believes that it is the ceo who has to be the guardian of the key principles by which an organization operates. "My message is a simple one," she told a reporter. "It is the reverse side of managing change. It is the protection of the few core values you have to stick to that are vital to your corporate culture—the things you would never compromise on." In other words, ceos and other business leaders need to distinguish between core competencies and core values. "Core competency is your knowledge," she explained. "Core value is your character." And that core value, according to Gadiesh's reasoning, "allows you to change, but stick to those important key principles at the same time. . . . this is a part of the ceo's job, to be a guardian of those values."[6]

Savage is employing the same tactics used by many ceos in turnaround situations. In such efforts, bringing in a new top manager may mean that the ax is surely going to fall. But it may also be the only way to achieve a new strategic orientation, one that results from a different background and set of experiences. Another advantage of the outsider-as-turnaround-leader is that the "new guy" can effect strategic change because he isn't saddled with personal commitments to the organization's hoary policies, mores, and procedures.

This "invented here" syndrome is often the reason that the previous management blames—as Davenport did—external and uncontrollable variables, such as rotten luck, for the organization's problems. Not surprisingly, a new management team is much more likely to identify internal and controllable variables as the direct causes of the crisis. Savage's behavior is thoroughly predictable given the situation the 918th faces. When replacing a failed leader, best to take firm control.

The first to go is the hapless Keith Davenport, whose command Savage dispatches instantly with the words "It's the group commander. Well, it's always the group commander. It's his job, isn't it?" when asked by General Pritchard to identify the cause of the 918th's troubles. Two demotions quickly follow. The first victim is a thoroughly stunned young enlisted clerk whom Savage demotes to private for being out of uniform. Next is the 918th's Air Executive Officer, Lieutenant Colonel Ben Gately (Hugh Marlowe), the son and grandson of two famous army generals, who receives a humiliating chewing out after he's been placed under arrest and brought to Savage's office. "You're not Air Exec anymore, you're just an airplane commander," growls Savage as the heavily perspiring Gately stands ramrod at attention. "And I want you to paint this name on the nose of your ship—"Leper Colony"—because in it you're going to get every deadbeat in the outfit. Every man with a penchant for head colds. If there's a bombardier who can't hit his plate with his fork, you get him. If there's a navigator who can't find the men's room, you get him, because you rate him. Is that clear?"

## Restructuring Challenges

Savage's methods are rash, not unlike the restructuring tactics that have become customary in corporate America, where wholesale replacement of management teams is often the method of choice to produce the fastest possible turnaround results in troubled companies.

Such tactics have, not surprisingly, generated a healthy discussion on how best to effect change in dysfunctional organizational cultures like that in the 918th. This preserve-or-replace debate has recently been described in a *Wall Street Journal* article on turnaround management. Preservationists argue that cleaning house often creates more problems than it solves—rebuilding morale, retraining, and recruiting can take up valuable time. Then there's the significant loss in productivity that inevitably comes when surviving employees dedicate themselves only to protecting their turf.

Better, the argument goes, to do as Louis V. Gerstner did at IBM and George Fisher did at Eastman Kodak: keep existing management in place. Better to change points of view than change people.

Replacement proponents, on the other hand, would support Savage's brash moves, arguing that a failing organization needs an ax-swinger. They cite the phenomenal success of Lucent

Technologies, whose management team consists primarily of replacements for the AT&T executives who ran the business before it was spun off. The philosophy at Lucent is that replacing senior executives is an agonizing but essential process. As one observer put it, "I can't think about any significant changes without significant importation of outside talent."[7]

Until he wins a few supporters, Savage is dealing with men who are still clinging to each other, worrying about their friends, their roommates, their old allegiances to a past leader. Savage offers them nothing to cling to but the mission. The men want to transfer out. So, how does the tide turn? It turns largely in a passive scene, in which Savage reveals to a young pilot his own vision of the mission.

This young pilot will go to bat for Savage and sway the entire group toward Savage's vision. From this point on, his squadron really gains its wings. And Savage does too, letting down his guard, if only to himself, enough to share the victories and losses of his men. And this—take note—is where his dilemma begins, a dilemma that only the observant Major Stovall detects. Frank Savage is as torn between the mission and the men as Davenport was, and, as Stovall points out, "The only difference between Frank Savage and Keith Davenport is that Savage is about that much taller."

How does Savage balance his affections, his increasingly specific concern for the individuals in his group? Not like Davenport. And General Pritchard makes certain of it:

| GENERAL SAVAGE | How do you know what you're pushing Gately into? How do you know we didn't send Bishop up just that once too often? I |
|---|---|

don't even know how I'll know, but I'm the one that's down there, and I'll have to . . .

General
Pritchard

Frank, you're swinging after the bell. Tell me something, will you? What was the name of the man you relieved?

General
Savage

Who, Keith?

General
Pritchard

What was his trouble, do you remember? You're not propping them up too, are you? Take a good look, Frank.

General
Savage

You think that?

General
Pritchard

It would be natural enough. The things you go through with a bunch of those boys, working your way out of the hole with them. It's hard not to let them get under your hide. And the one thing I've noticed on the record lately, you've been flying *more* missions rather than less.

Warned, Savage will swing the other way dramatically, pushing aside every emotion that assails him, keeping his strength and stoicism in the front line for his men to witness. He'll be the unbreakable backbone of the group. His choice keeps his men on their feet, full of pride and fight, but Savage also swallows his own responses for the good of the group, or to preserve his authority. You find yourself hoping that he'll come through with a moment of revealed sentiment, but there are few such moments. And the more losses he suffers, the more he'll press forward.

Afraid of becoming another Keith Davenport, Savage takes a successful stance a bit too far. He's no longer just a rock-hard winner; he's in a personal lock-up that keeps everyone and everything out. Another friend dead? "Well, that's the way it goes!" he barks with a shrug, and Stovall, disgusted, mouths "Maximum . . . maximum effort" with the irony of a genuine seer who knows that Savage's maximum effort is nearly complete, and its end will include an emotional break equal to Keith Davenport's.

"I'm confused," Stovall reports succinctly, then lists pointedly for Savage the names of the men—friends, colleagues—who have died. They are the casualties of a war, true, but Savage is just a bit too casual about them, and even Davenport frowns in dismay at Savage's fiercely brusque manner.

Nevertheless, a pattern for dealing with failed teams begins to emerge:

1. **Make incremental improvements.** General Savage, after analyzing the problems facing the 918th, realized that the rebuilding process would take time and numerous iterations. As a result, he identified primary levers of performance and then went "back to the fundamentals," starting with practice bombing runs and improving the group's formation flying. Only when the 918th had successfully climbed each rung of this

ladder did he lead them to the next level. What he was after, clearly, was a moderate but continuous improvement in performance, and he got it.

2. **Shock and refocus.** General Savage also knew that time available for these incremental changes was precious, and that the 918th had to transform itself substantially before its bombing effectiveness could improve. His dramatic actions early after arriving at the group (reorganizing staff, closing the bar at the officers' club, reassigning roommates, creating the "Leper Colony") were designed to shake things up, to get everyone's attention, and to signal that, under his leadership, mission success and the group—not individual concerns—would be all-important.

3. **Embrace a higher aspiration.** Savage invested a great deal of energy in getting people to raise their sights. He instilled in the 918th a true sense of purpose (daylight low-level precision bombing) that provided its members with a reason for being. (Remember, Keith Davenport could not define maximum effort nor could he communicate the 918th's purpose.) This went beyond just a sense of mission and vision and made the flyers actually eager to fly their assignments.

4. **Grow new leaders.** Exceptional leaders help to create new leaders. Savage knew that everyone in the 918th needed to manifest leadership, no matter what job they had. He saw this as particularly important because his was a military organization in which communications could quickly be cut off and a single leader could easily be lost.

5. **Remember that organizational transformation must initially be leader-driven.** Experts who study effective turn-

arounds have discovered something: at its inception, real change is almost always the result of one person's focus, tenacity, and drive. At this stage of a turnaround, the leader's singlehanded direction-setting, energy, and laserlike commitment to change must overcome the inertia that so often defines the underperforming organization. Most typically, the leader invokes a crisis, as Savage did, to get the organization to adopt a new operating model. Only later does the leader relinquish power to others in the organization and give up top-down change efforts to continue the turnaround process. Timing is everything here, knowing when to move to broad-based, bottom-up performance improvements that would get everyone—even the ground echelon personnel—to take a new approach to their jobs, thereby fully institutionalizing the transformation.

6. **Make sure you have the right stuff.** Studies of successful turnarounds reveal important behaviors of the leaders who led them. They were quick studies, capable of sizing up a situation instantly. They were objective. They had the courage to take painful but indispensable steps, even without complete information. They set an example for others. They communicated well.

Successful turnarounds, like that of the 918th Bomber Group, are tough but doable. Take the case of another, less bellicose air force, the commercial jets of Continental Airlines. This once first-rate airline had, in 1994, hit rock bottom, losing more than $200 million after two bankruptcies and a revolving-door series of ten CEOs over as many years. Things had become so embarrassing that the company's mechanics removed Continental logos from their uniforms so that they wouldn't be recognized—and ridiculed—on their way home from work. Executives stopped going to parties where they knew jokes would be made about the company's famously bad service. "This airline was probably, candidly, one of the least-respected airlines in corporate America," a spokesperson told a reporter. "You could not get any worse than Continental in 1994."[8]

Simply put, Continental had become the 918th Bomber Group of commercial aviation. Enter new CEO Gordon Bethune, who captured skeptical employees with the motto *From worst to first* soon after firing or demoting nearly every vice president in the company and cutting the survivors' pay. Bethune, who's also a licensed jet pilot, then directed his focus to making sure that everyone in the company understood his goals and their role in achieving them. To drive this point home, he put his money where his mouth was by paying every employee $65 for each month Continental ranked in the top five airlines for on-time performance and $100 for each month it was in first place. And he insisted on reducing the bureaucracy, going so far as to stage a parking lot incineration of Continental's stodgy 800-page policy and procedures manual to make his point.

The result was one of the quickest and most successful turnarounds in the airline industry. By 1996, a short two years after Bethune arrived on the scene, Continental was ranked top in service, pay was brought back to pre-1994 levels, and profits surged to $556 million. What's more, in 1997 the airline was ranked as the number-one major airline in customer satisfaction by J. D. Power and Associates.

So, too, the 918th is turned around—a leper colony becomes a fierce squadron of first-rate bombers, and every man is raised to the highest standard. But then suddenly, alarmingly, consummate leader Frank Savage loses his strength. He can't even pull himself up into the airplane. He freezes and descends into a catatonic state from which no one can shake him:

| | |
|---|---|
| COLONEL DAVENPORT | Whaddya make of it? |
| DOC | State of shock. Complete collapse. Everything let go at once. |
| MAJOR STOVALL | Can't you give him a hypo, Doc, something to knock him out, put him to sleep? |
| DOC | No, in his present condition it wouldn't be any good. He's somewhere up there with the mission. When they get back, maybe he'll let go. I hope. |
| COLONEL DAVENPORT | It's screwy! I wouldn't ever figure it could happen to him! |
| MAJOR STOVALL | I did. I watched him sweep his feelings under the carpet long enough! It had to spill out someday. |
| COLONEL DAVENPORT | But I never saw him more full of fight than he was at briefing! |
| DOC | Have you ever seen a light bulb burn out? How bright the filament is just before it lets go? I think they call it *maximum effort*. |

Though Frank Savage had sworn not to "carry" his men as Keith Davenort did, he's ended up carrying that and more—the weight of his own imperative to conceal both from his men and from himself what he's had to give up in order to lead. The conclusion seems inescapable. Frank Savage has gotten too much into his role, that "mask of command" we referred to earlier, that so effectively can disguise the human psyche behind it.

No wonder Harvey Stovall's insightful remark, "I've watched him sweep his feelings under the carpet," seems both totally reasonable and totally absurd. Of course, Savage has tried too hard to remain stoic, an impenetrable fort of strength, and in this era that champions "felt" experience, his collapse seems logical. He should have allowed himself a little more humanity, a moment's nod toward his own losses, letting the mask slip a bit so others can begin to discover the vulnerable actor beneath.

The tragedy of *Twelve O'Clock High* is that Frank Savage has successfully led his men but has become a casualty himself. This is the final touch of war. Maximum effort in this context, it turns out, has costs, a fitting reminder that there are limits to performance even the most ambitious of leaders could one day meet.

# PART FOUR

# SELF-LEADERSHIP

*Charles Foster Kane (Orson Welles) makes more empty promises in*
Citizen Kane.

# EIGHT

# WHEN LEADERSHIP FAILS

## *Citizen Kane*

### CAST OF CHARACTERS

Charles Foster Kane *(Orson Welles)*

Jedediah Leland *(Joseph Cotten)*

Susan Alexander *(Dorothy Comingore)*

Jim Gettys *(Ray Collins)*

Mrs. Kane *(Agnes Moorehead)*

Director: Orson Welles

Screenwriters: Herman J. Mankiewicz and Orson Welles

In the surreal opening sequences of *Citizen Kane*, you are made to feel unwelcome, a member of an audience that is somehow in the wrong theater. The camera slowly pans up from a dilapidated NO TRESPASSING sign hanging from a rusting chain-link fence. A slow dissolve reveals a cast-iron gate that seems to forbid your entrance. The funereal music, part bass viol and part synthesizer, suggests impregnability and unfathomable secrets. In the deep distance, its spires rising through low-hanging clouds, a mansion guarded by ramparts slowly comes into focus, one light emanating from its many windows. There is no way to penetrate this forbidden place. No way, that is, until the camera—apparently with a mind of its own— slowly passes over the gate.

We enter the bedroom of a dying man. Grainy black-and-white newsreels, reminiscent of another era, chronicle his very public story of travel, mystery, women, and politics, all the accoutrements of a great fortune. But the standard biography seems tauntingly incomplete. This void is neatly filled by the appearance of a newspaper reporter who sets out to expose the dying man's complete story. We become unwitting voyeurs on this journey, probing for a solution to the puzzle that is the life of Charles Foster Kane.

The journey is well worth making. *Citizen Kane* was a movie so artistically and technically advanced when produced in 1941, it was—and is today—a veritable textbook for budding auteurs. (The most recent tribute of a young filmmaker to *Citizen Kane* is Todd Haynes's 1998 film *Velvet Goldmine*, in which the Kane figure is a rock superstar; and film editor Walter Murch has devoted himself to honoring Welles's masterful techniques by recutting the director's last film, *Touch of Evil* [1958], as Welles intended it to be cut.)

Even the lighting techniques of *Citizen Kane* mark the film as innovative and masterful. They brilliantly illuminate the protagonist's enthusiastic and entrepreneurial youth, producing almost no shadowing; yet as the tragic story unfolds, this sunny clarity is replaced by dismal light-dark contrasts.

The effect is telling. As one film scholar puts it, in *Citizen Kane* "what is concealed is often more important than what's revealed."[1] Then there's that persistent music, its repeated notes conjuring an ever-shifting array of moods as Kane's life careens from optimism to gloom. The cinematography is remarkable— deep-focus shots that make both foreground and distant planes visible; wide-angle shots that emphasize both visual distance and psychological separation; camera movements that imply both energy and lassitude; shots angled from the floor (Welles dug trenches for those) to glorify a character's stature. And finally, marvelous "wipes" take one image off the screen while seamlessly replacing it with another, used to great effect in portraying the progressive deterioration of Kane's first marriage.

*Citizen Kane* is on every critic's list of all-time great films. "For the first time on the screen we have seen the equivalent of a novel by Dos Passos," rhapsodized André Barzin. "Welles's first and best, a film that broke all the rules and invented some new ones," declared Leonard Maltin. "The greatest movie of all time," wrote Roger Ebert. Bob Stephens wrote in the *San Francisco Examiner*: "*Citizen Kane* has the best of everything. A great director and star, innovative cinematography, dream-like—even nightmarish—art direction, a sonorous musical score, a skillful screenplay in which comic passages intensify the movie's tragic qualities by means of their grotesque juxtaposition (how lifelike!), a psychological/narrative form that predates our contemporary 'psycho-histories' by at least 40 years, and best of all, a memorial word that, when spoken, recalls the film out of thin air."[2]

## The Mysterious "Rosebud"

That word is *Rosebud*; heard early in the film, it is Kane's last utterance. Perhaps it symbolizes his childhood innocence. Yet, as one of the characters observes late in the film, "I don't think any word can explain a man's life. No, I guess *Rosebud* is just a piece in a jigsaw puzzle—a missing piece."

Whatever it symbolizes, it is an unabashed attention-getter, so potent that anyone who has seen *Citizen Kane* cannot help but join in this search for meaning. Watch this film and you will be hooked. Search for—and find or fail to find—your own *Rosebud*, and you will be enriched.

But there's more here than masterful filmography. *Citizen Kane* also has much to teach us about the sometimes volatile trajectory of leadership and the ways in which power can at first create and then later corrupt. All the ingredients of a great story are in place. We answer with the protagonist his call to adventure, witness his confrontations, join him in the "underworld" where his rite of passage becomes our own nightmare, then judge him at his trials. And we will be with him when he confronts death.

*Citizen Kane* is the story of a man of immense talent, creativity, ambition, and energy whose life and career, once so full of potential, end as do many hero quests: tragically. Here is Peter Drucker's monomaniac-with-a-mission, the crusading entrepreneur whose noble desire to build ends up destroying. Kane, as obsessed as Ahab, is the charismatic teambuilder who ultimately fails because of arrogance. No wonder that, in the end, Charles Foster Kane becomes a "citizen" without *civitas*, an isolated and friendless outsider whose allegiance is only to himself.

Charles Foster Kane is a classic failed leader. Watching the dervish of young Charlie Kane whirl into big business, filled with conviction, talent, clear principles, and a far-reaching vision, is inspiration for any rising leader. Observing Kane's vigor become obsession, his talent become manipulation, the principles fade into a yellowed antique, and the man himself stagger and fall under the weight of his own gross errors is sure to sober anyone summoning the courage to lead.

## Failed Promise

No other film in history needs the story of its creators to teach its more startling lessons. *Citizen Kane* does. Why? Because Charles Kane's failure to fulfill his youthful promise is only one note in a dirge for failed promise that includes the story of director Orson Welles, the boy genius of Hollywood, and of William Randolph Hearst, the most powerful publisher in the world.

Both of these men are linked to Kane's career trajectory. Some say the film is about Hearst; some insist the film is about Welles; some argue that Kane is simply Kane, the product—as is any artistic creation—of imagination and influence. But Kane is all three identities. Pull at one thread, and you unravel the tapestry of tales.

The leadership tales of these men, like the story of *Citizen Kane*, begin at their end. Say the name of director, actor, producer, and writer Orson Welles, and most film and television viewers will not see in their mind's eye the young Welles arriving in Hollywood, fresh and eager. Instead, they see Welles as he was shortly before his death in 1986, appearing pretentious and comic in commercials as he pushed products, or in interviews as obese and paranoid, babbling about past career injustices. As his own life drew to a close, Welles came across as bereft of creative power.

It's a tragic end to a life so promising. Fade in on Welles, age 14, writing, directing, and starring in some thirty plays at his school in Illinois; or Welles, age 25, founder and director of the popular Mercury Theatre Radio Troupe, producing a live broadcast of H. G. Wells's sci-fi classic *War of the Worlds* so realistic that listeners packed up their belongings and fled to escape the aliens they believed had landed; or Welles in July of 1939, at age 26, negotiating and signing an unprecedented film contract with the major motion picture studio RKO Pictures that granted him complete artistic control of a film. Welles would approve the film's final cut, so long as he stayed within his $500,000 budget. He'd never made a movie. He'd never been to Hollywood. But he'd earned the name *boy wonder* and he led a loyal team, his Mercury Theatre Players, whom he brought with him to Hollywood.

His reputation as a talented theatrical leader and his determination to give his players and technicians artistic freedom gathered more film artists to him. And so, the story goes, he pursued the project of his dreams, setting up camp like Kane in his first bustling news office.

Here was a bright man with a bright future; and, like most embarking leaders, he was unconcerned with—or even unaware of—the paradoxes in his own nature that had the power to ultimately ruin his achievements.

Likewise, William Randolph Hearst, the journalist and millionaire whose life also inspired *Citizen Kane*, showed great promise as a young leader. But in the end, few words have been more frequently applied to this powerful and controversial newspaper tycoon than *paradoxical*. His beliefs and actions seemed always at odds with one another—illogical at best, hypocritical at worst. Hearst's name now provokes contempt and judgment. *Yellow journalism*—a term coined for Hearst's style of newspapering—has now become synonymous with sensationalistic, underhanded reporting.

But the young Hearst burst into big business with a terrific energy and the freedom to make grand decisions and enact them fearlessly, thanks to his considerable wealth. Hearst's early fortune, inherited from his senator father, granted him, literally, a blank check to move, change, inspire, wield power, and succeed without constraints—much as Welles's own talents had gained him a personal "blank check" in Hollywood. Hearst's early enthusiasm gave little indication of his deeper paradoxes, which would ultimately define and distort his leadership.

To study the making of *Citizen Kane* is to discover the unchecked, paradoxical personalities of three men.

## The Entrepreneurial Psyche

Manfred Kets de Vries, professor of management at INSEAD in Fontainebleau, France, has carefully studied these ambiguities, the paradoxical "internal psychic theater," as he calls it, of the entrepreneur. There is first, he reports, the altogether positive side of the entrepreneurial spirit: achievement orientation, a desire to take responsibility for decisions, incredibly high energy, huge perseverance and imagination, willingness to take risks, and contagious enthusiasm. "Whatever it is," writes Kets de Vries, "—seductiveness, gamesmanship, or charisma—entrepreneurs somehow know how to lead an organization and give it momentum."[3]

But then there is the dark side. Entrepreneurs, he reports, are driven by the need to control, a tendency that can easily turn them into Kane-like misfits who have no tolerance for subordinates who want to think for themselves. This, when combined with distrust of the world around them (as is frequently the case), can cause entrepreneurs to create organizations in which sycophants rule, employees cease to think for themselves, and political maneuvering is widespread.

Kets de Vries must have been studying Charles Foster Kane or William Randolph Hearst when he reported that the entrepreneur's unbridled need for approval often leads to the construction of monuments as symbols of their achievement, which any *Citizen Kane* viewer might call the Xanadu complex.

The question here is, To what degree can a leader foresee the complexities of his or her own nature enough to save himself or herself from fatal missteps?

Certainly there are plenty of people to pat you on the back—people who will remind you that power can make you giddy, process is more valuable than profit, to keep "a good head on your shoulders," and that "the road to hell is paved with gold." The problem is, most people have *two* selves, and usually don't know it—and never know it when it matters most. F. Scott Fitzgerald—the American novelist known for his keen characterizations of rising businessmen and famous for his ability to discern critical weakness and error in both himself and others—believed that "the test of a first rate intelligence is the ability to hold two opposed ideas in the mind at the same time and still retain the ability to function."[4]

Charles Foster Kane, who is grandly inoperative by the end of *Citizen Kane*, is a real charmer in the early scenes of this film, much like the men who helped create him. Screenwriter Herman Mankiewicz pulled from his firsthand experiences with both Hearst and the dynamic young Welles to conceive this early and healthfully entrepreneurial Kane—smart and ambitious, yes, but also comfortable with people, amiable, quick-witted, a natural organizer of teams.

He assumes control easily and knows how to enjoy his work. He wants fun for himself and for his staff, and he knows how to generate the office excitement that surrounds a common goal. He has a vision, and principles he intends to uphold. These he offers up as a clear Declaration of Principles, a manifesto, an early version of what we might now call a mission statement, delivered on the front page of one of his early newspapers.

> KANE  There's something I've got to get into this paper besides pictures and print. I've got to make the *New York Inquirer* as important to New York as the gas in that light.

> LELAND  What're you going to do, Charlie?

> KANE  Declaration of Principles. Don't smile, Jedediah. Got it all written out: Declaration of Principles.

> BERNSTEIN  You don't want to make any promises, Mr. Kane, you don't want to keep.

> KANE  These'll be kept. "I'll provide the people of this city with a daily paper that will tell all the news honestly. I will also provide them . . ."

> LELAND  That's the second sentence you started with "I" . . .

> KANE  People are going to know who's responsible. And they're going to get the truth in the *Inquirer* quickly and simply and entertainingly, and no special interests are going to be allowed to interfere with that truth. "I'll also

provide them with a fighting and tireless
champion of their rights as citizens and as
human beings."

One of his employees, Jedediah Leland (Joseph Cotten),
requests this statement as a memento: "I'd like to keep that particular piece of paper myself," he says. "I have a hunch it might
turn out to be something pretty important. A document, like
the Declaration of Independence, and the Constitution, and
my first report card at school."

## The Missing Mission Statement

No wonder. It's noble stuff to light the way, to focus Kane
Enterprises' staff and employees and to establish their accountability to its readers. But mission statements, once written, can
all too easily be shelved, or casually discarded and forgotten
like yesterday's newspaper.

Or, even worse, they are just puffery, meaningless phrases
that soon become more *ad*mission than mission. Who hasn't
read one of these, something like, "Our mission is to endeavor
to achieve outstanding performance and better our customers'
lives through our service-driven, customer-focused products
and services"?

Not surprisingly, James Krohe, Jr., who studies such managerial arcana, has concluded that Kane-like mission statements
may mean very little. He finds, in fact, that no link exists
between the adoption of a mission statement and subsequent
company performance. Krohe cites research done by the

London-based Institute of Personnel and Development among fifteen multinational companies, including such luminaries as Texas Instruments and Johnson & Johnson.

The disarming results of that research suggested that companies that have no mission statement often had the most profound sense of mission. So much for one of management's newest fads!

Most pointedly, Krohe seems to have Charles Foster Kane in mind when he suggests that "seeing your words emblazoned on wallet cards and posters in the cafeteria is heady stuff, as is hearing them quoted approvingly at meetings by eager acolytes. No wonder the average CEO deduces that he has made converts to the faith by sheer eloquence, forgetting that cheering anything the boss says is as natural to the employees as sleeping is to a cat. Mission statements thus confirm the vanity of the boss who assumes that when things go right, it is because of something he did."[5]

There is a kind of tectonic shift that can take place between the solemn invocation and the implementation of a mission statement. Sure, it's the leader's job to get people to share a vision—but it's daily actions, not flowery speech, that vivify it. If you doubt this, simply reread Kane's manifesto at the end of the film and you'll have trouble knowing what he is talking about.

## The Beginning of Greatness

At first, Kane's obsessions seem almost healthy. He is, after all, an entrepreneur on the make, driven to increase circulation for his newly purchased paper by publishing the sensational and confrontational and by concocting phony stories to gain public attention. He's doing what every startup leader must do—spend money to make money. In these early stages, his staff sees and supports his clear intention—to raise the newspaper from the dust and to secure its financial success. More important, Kane reveals considerable self-knowledge in a discussion with his banker:

> KANE  The trouble is, you don't realize you're talking to two people. As Charles Foster Kane, who owns 82,364 shares of Public Transit Preferred (you see, I do have a general idea of my holdings) I sympathize with you. Charles Foster Kane is a scoundrel. His paper should be run out of town. A committee should be formed to boycott him. You may, if you can form such a committee, put me down for a contribution of $1,000. On the other hand, I am the publisher of the *Inquirer*. As such, it's my duty (and I'll let you in on a little secret, it's also my pleasure) to see to it that decent, hardworking people in this community aren't robbed blind by a pack of money-mad pirates just because they haven't anybody to look after their interests. . . . I think I'm the man to do it. You see, I have money and property.

This scene is a reminder that Charlie's success as a young man is founded on his ability to control *himself*—not on his ability to control others.

## The Welles-Kane Connection

Orson Welles was able to recognize a similar psychic duality in himself when he admitted to his biographer Kenneth Tynan, "Everything about me is a contradiction, and so is everything about everybody else. We are made out of oppositions; we live between two poles. There's a philistine and an aesthete in all of us, and a murderer and a saint. You don't reconcile the poles. You just recognize them."

Certainly Welles's career—after that first frenzy of success and reputed promise—quickly became a battle between his gifts and his own arrogance, which the Hollywood community was quick to use against him. There were apparent weaknesses in Welles's nature, which he seemed unable to control and which caused turbulence and unrest among his coworkers and, worse, among the authorities at RKO Pictures.

He had, for instance, a penchant for tantrums when others disagreed with him—tantrums of such magnitude that they inspired Mankiewicz to write Kane's room-trashing rage as a final scene in *Citizen Kane*. Welles also had a tendency to take credit for other people's ideas, and he had a sense of power, many report, that was so megalomaniacal that he earned a reputation as a man in rivalry with God. It was Mankiewicz who remarked acidly, if wittily, as Welles walked by, "There but for the grace of God goes God."

Sadly, the more opposition Welles faced in Hollywood, the more arrogant and profligate he is said to have become, utterly unable to see his own defiant behavior clearly. "He was great!" cries *Citizen Kane* set designer Sam Leve in a documentary on the making of the film. "And the greatness drove him down to nothingness!" Why? "Because he was careless."[6]

Probably everyone concurs that Welles was also professionally tormented and ruined by Hearst, who made the destruction of Orson Welles his business. Welles was denied artistic freedom on his subsequent film contracts before *Citizen Kane* had even been released; he lost the trust and backing of everyone in a position to finance his visions; and he would fight against Hearst and Hollywood, futilely and for the rest of his life, to regain his power and position. But, to his credit, Welles acknowledged the role his own inconsistencies and erratic behavior played in his decline. He clearly saw his conflicting impulses fighting for autonomy: "You don't reconcile the poles. You just recognize them." And hope that when you do, it's not too late.

The irony here is that Welles was so ruthless in *Citizen Kane* in criticizing the very dichotomies—so much like his own— that he saw in millionaire William Randolph Hearst.

## The Hearst-Kane Connection

By 1912, Hearst's nature was apparent. He was unable to succeed in the political arena he coveted, and he had become, for most, a joke, the stupefyingly wealthy victim of his own grasping, imperial willfulness—a victim of himself. Nothing besides *Citizen Kane* reveals so glaringly the self-aggrandizing Hearst as does his personal palace near the tiny town of San Simeon, California. This is Hearst Castle, the gaudily grotesque aerie built by Hearst in the 1920s. This is no paradise, no enchanted hill, no quaint ranch. Here a visitor comes not upon Shangri-La, but upon what one observer wisely called "your crazy uncle's attic, half the size of Rhode Island." Hearst Castle is a rotting mausoleum. It is the archaeology of its builder's affectations and lavish acquisitiveness, helping to bring his grasping life into focus, a life that just had to become a movie.

This spectacle was the home of the self-appointed king who called himself "the voice of the common man." No wonder that, near the end of his life, all the paradoxes of Hearst's career were endlessly pondered by biographers. Hearst reacted to these biographies as if he were two men, unable to reconcile: "If it doesn't tell the truth, it will make me mad, and if it tells the truth, it will make me sad."[7]

Not surprisingly, Welles was fascinated by this ultimate paradox of the entrepreneur, the wily businessperson who must destroy in order to create.

## The Beginning of Failure

As viewers of Kane's story, you are probably painfully sure that something is failing in Charlie Kane's wonderful, charismatic nature. Most of what you witness in this film after its first few scenes of youthful vigor is:

- A depiction of Kane's *surrender* of self-awareness and abandonment of self-control for the control of others— his staff, his friends, his wives, and finally, the public he claims to represent
- His denial of those on his staff who remind him of his "better" self—especially Leland, a close friend from Kane's youth and witness to his transformation

- His willing drift from the principles and mission designed by that better self—he chooses quantity over quality, political abandonment of the common workers and of honesty, decency, and equal representation
- A preference for illusion over reality—the pretense of friendship, the fantasy of romantic love, empty gestures of generosity toward the public and his staff
- His insistent subversion of the goals of others, as he replaces group and individual ambition with his own (for example, controlling his wife's career)

In short, you observe the results of one leader's inability to hold two opposing truths—or selves—in mind at once as he becomes more powerful.

Such growing monomania has often been plotted on the predictable trajectory of power misused. James McGregor Burns, who rightly is credited with inventing the field of leadership studies, labeled this dictatorial tendency *power wielding*. Such a relationship between leader (or should we say *tyrant*) and followers is based on a kind of psychological control of others, an instrumental approach to leadership that reduces followers to objects and forces them to assume subservient roles. The leader's ego and need for power smothers others, replacing influence with coercion. *Citizen Kane* may have dissected William Randolph Hearst's hypocritical power, but it also foreshadowed much of Welles's imminent career struggles; and ultimately, the story of Charles Foster Kane and of his two progenitors is a triple threat to an aspiring leader: Know thyself!

Or else be consumed by power. That engine of leadership can be a great motivator, or it can corrode. Kane's, Welles's, and

Hearst's unmistakable need for power and the impulse to influence others are the perfectly normal attributes of an effective leader. They are, in fact, remarkably reliable predictors of success.

Yet they must be checked. The key is to ensure that power and influence is directed toward the good of the organization, not the individual. This paradoxical nature of power has been studied by researchers, who have discovered that leaders are motivated by three urgent needs: the need for achievement (to do something better or more efficiently than before), the need for affiliation (establishing or maintaining friendly relations with others), and the need for power (to have an impact on others).[8] All of this seems perfectly benign until we learn that it is the need for power that predominates in the successful leader. That's a positive force when it benefits the institution, but a disaster when it benefits the leader.

## Problems Back at the Office

Of course it is Kane's stunning success that precipitates his ultimate failure. As his media empire's revenue and profits build, things inevitably begin to spin out of control. Kane's business is in a phase that management scholar and "organizational therapist" Ichak Adizes calls *Prime*.[9] It's growing rapidly, aggressively devastating all competitors, assembling a "portfolio" of robust subdivisions—newspapers, radio stations. It is at the top of its life cycle. Kane seems to be an early version of Ted Turner and Rupert Murdoch combined. He controls the market; he *is* the media. But his organization is so hierarchical, so dominated by his personality, so top-down, that no one is managing. As a result, Kane's kingdom is crumbling, moving from "prime" to second-rate. Feelings of invincibility, it seems, have a way of coming home to roost. Lest you think it only happens in the movies, consider the warning signs that Adizes's research has revealed:

- The company never seems to have enough of the kind of talent it needs, and it is engaged in a continuous search for more and better people.
- There is a lack of awareness that the aging process begins in Prime. Management must take action to retard the aging process while the company is still in Prime.
- The headquarters staff gains more and more authority, which it takes from increasingly disempowered staff on the line.
- The finance and legal departments become more powerful than marketing and sales.
- The finance department makes budgets, which top management approves and then delegates to the heads of divisions.
- Rewards are based on short-term results only.
- Only a minority of the company's stockholders, if any, are company employees.
- Relying on past successes, the company depends on its tried-and-true lines. Only a small portion of revenues comes from products that did not exist three years ago.

- Decision making is centralized in the leader.
- The organization depends on a single leader for its development and growth.
- With no clear mission, the company repeats the past rather than inventing the future.

Watching Charlie Kane mishandle power is both troubling and embarrassing for the viewer: is he *really* in error when he pirates another newspaper's best reporters for himself? Surely it's the staff of the *Chronicle* that's at fault here, so easily bought! But it's clear that this leader takes more pride in purchase than in principles and that he has little concern about the deeper convictions and commitments of his team. On what foundation will his team flourish, if their principles are so irrelevant to the leader? That question, of course, begs another: what *are* Charlie's principles?

They seem to be changing. Leland expresses his concern as any loyal team member might—tentatively, quietly, and with some self-doubt: "Am I a stuffed shirt? Am I a horse-faced hypocrite? Am I a New England schoolmarm?" No, he is a truthteller.

## The Importance of Naysayers

In time, Leland abandons his doubts and becomes Kane's accuser, as well as a private memory bank for Kane, always on hand to remind him of early ideals and goals and of the identity Kane consistently fails to choose.

Leland is the embodiment of that rare and hugely valuable person in the organization who is its conscience, its devil's advocate, its naysayer. But, of course, we often shoot such truthtellers. That's tragic, since they're rarely motivated by selfishness, but instead, like Leland, by a real commitment to the organization's avowed principles and mission.

Charles Foster Kane's sad career trajectory would be irrelevant if we did not so clearly see ourselves in its shadows. No wonder we, and millions of film viewers, have paid so much attention to his story. *Citizen Kane* reminds us that there are predictable seasons, or *cycles* in a career. When these rhythms are as tragic as Kane's, they can serve as helpful guides to an essentially unknowable future.

When *Citizen Kane* comes to its end, and we are left with its last image of *Rosebud*—perhaps his lost youth—it is impossible not to think of the ends of the men who created him: Hearst and Welles. Hearst's own life is wrapped up succinctly by Simon Callow in *Orson Welles: The Road to Xanadu*:

Heir to a mining fortune, after a profligate youth, [Hearst] had sought elected office without ever once coming close; abandoning the ballot box, he had used his fortune to buy up a chain of newspapers, through whose pages he then promoted his political beliefs. . . . He had rapidly developed from a progressive to a fascist, consorting with Hitler and Mussolini; as a man, he had developed from a high-spirited anti-authoritarian prankster (he had been business manager of the Harvard

*Lampoon*) into a crusty and pompous reactionary, using the American League of Decency to disseminate his anti-Communist, pro-family views in twenty-eight newspapers, thirteen magazines and on two radio stations. In rather naked contrast to this, he lived, very publicly but unreported, with his mistress Marion Davies. Just as he attempted to control American public opinion by sheer will power and money, he attempted to turn Davies from a delightful and accomplished comedienne into the biggest star in Hollywood. Buying a studio in which to make starring vehicles for her, orchestrating frenzies of excitement at their premiers, and then having them reviewed in apocalyptic terms, he succeeded only in making the films, Miss Davies, and himself ridiculous.[10]

Ridiculous. Hardly the legacy or eulogy Hearst dreamed of. Ironically, Hearst is immortalized most memorably as Charles Foster Kane, the very depiction he hoped most to suppress.

And Welles? He eulogized himself in a 1982 interview: "I think I made a mistake, essentially, staying in movies. It's a mistake I can't regret because it's like saying, I shouldn't have stayed married to that woman, but I did because I love her. I would have been more successful if I'd left movies, stayed in theater, gone into politics, written *anything*. I've wasted the greater part of my life looking for money and trying to get along. . . . It's 2 percent movie making and 98 percent hustling. It's no way to spend a life."[11]

Here is Leland, eulogizing Charles Foster Kane:

LELAND  Not that Charlie was ever brutal. He just did brutal things. Maybe I wasn't his friend. But if I wasn't, he never had one. . . . He had a generous mind. I don't suppose anybody ever had so many opinions. But he never believed in anything except Charlie Kane. He never had a conviction except Charlie Kane in his life. I supposed he died without one. Must have been pretty unpleasant.

Can we fade out on these three figures, each somehow incomplete without the other's influence, and all bound together by their rise and fall, by their enormous errors of ego, and ultimately, all losers of the public support they had seemed so sure to win?

We cannot. Though the careers of Welles, Hearst, and Kane ended sadly, *Citizen Kane* has endured—as art, as biography, as autobiography, or as all three—a gesture of promise that serves now as an epitaph to the lives of failed leaders.

*Bud Fox (Charlie Sheen) ponders the ethics of Gordon Gekko's (Michael Douglas) advice that "greed is good" in* Wall Street.

# NINE

# MORALITY AND LEADERSHIP
## *Wall Street*

### CAST OF CHARACTERS

Gordon Gekko  *(Michael Douglas)*

Bud Fox  *(Charlie Sheen)*

Carl Fox  *(Martin Sheen)*

Lou Mannheim  *(Hal Holbrook)*

Darien Taylor  *(Daryl Hannah)*

Director: Oliver Stone

Screenwriters: Stanley Weiser and Oliver Stone

*. . . Greed, for lack of a better word, is good. Greed is right. Greed works. Greed clarifies, cuts through, and captures the essence of the evolutionary spirit. Greed, in all of its forms—greed for life, for money, for love, knowledge—has marked the upward surge of mankind. And greed, you mark my words, will not only save Teldar Paper, but that other malfunctioning corporation called the U.S. of A.*

**Gordon Gekko,** *Wall Street*

Film has generally not been kind to American business and the money culture that drives it. From *Cash McCall* (1959), in which James Garner played a slick turnaround artist who bought failing companies low and resold them high, to *Other People's Money* (1991), which pitted a crass, corrupt, and wildly hilarious Danny DeVito against the irreproachably noble Gregory Peck, movies have relentlessly mocked the businessperson. *How to Succeed in Business Without Really Trying* (1967) spoofed office politics and the long climb up the corporate ladder, while, more recently, the film adaptation of David Mamet's *Glengarry Glen Ross* (1992) brought the harried lucklessness of selling real estate in a down market to its stunned audiences. *Roger and Me* (1985) brutally dissed Roger Smith, the chairman of General Motors, after he had neutron-bombed Flint, Michigan, by closing plants and moving much of the giant automaker's production offshore. Producer, director, and self-professed corporate avenger Michael Moore stalked Smith for two years while creating a new pie-in-the-face film genre, docu-fiction. The nasty got nastier in Moore's *The Big One* (1997), a movie that beats up on the "scum" of corporate America, from a Payday candy factory to Borders and Nike. Finally, *Jerry Maguire* (1996) invented new rap ridicule for the art of the deal: "Show me the money!"

Movies, so often the target of criticism themselves, have shown a unique contempt for—and, at the same time, made quite a fortune from—that fulcrum of the capitalistic system, free enterprise.

Perhaps the negative spin that movies so regularly take on business is due to the fact that familiarity breeds contempt. After all, the movie industry is a robust artifact of the very money-grubbing system it so often pans. Or maybe it is because everyone loves a good Horatio Alger story gone wrong. Certainly, the business cycle can turn a high jump into a pratfall. And who can resist a modern Greek tragedy, a tale about a young man who, by pluck and good fortune, rises from his working-class station to earn a respectable job and the hope of a better life and piles of money—and then loses everything?

If that young man just happens to be recent college graduate Bud Fox (Charlie Sheen), a young hotshot stockbroker trying to build his "book" on Wall Street, so much the better. Fox, who believes *Fortune* magazine is the Bible, is the perfect wonderboy wannabe of the 1980s, the Decade of Greed, a time when almost everything—ethics, ideals, and even honesty— was sacrificed in pursuit of The Hot Deal. He's one of two protagonists in the 1987 movie *Wall Street*, the story of his meteroric rise and his soul-revealing fall.

Together, Fox and his idol, Gordon Gekko (Michael Douglas), provide convincing illustration of the 1980s, a time when sleaze and insider trading had more to do with stock values than the "fundamentals."

*Wall Street* is the creation of director Oliver Stone, whose movies *Platoon* (1986), *Born on the Fourth of July* (1989), *JFK* (1991), *Heaven and Earth* (1993), *Natural Born Killers* (1994), and *Nixon* (1995) have made him, as one observer put it, America's "controversial and volatile cultural messenger."[1] Stone, who himself is the son of a stockbroker, is uniquely able to capture Wall Street's lapses on film. He also consulted with an army of real-life Wall Street icons, including takeover specialist Asher Edelman; Dennis Block, a prominent deal lawyer; two government investigators who broke the famous Ivan Boesky case; an official from the Securities and Exchange Commission; and a sharp federal prosecutor.

Stone himself, it's worth noting, is a fascinating paradox whose methods as a hard-driving director create both turbulence and effective results. An interviewer once asked Stone about his rumored confrontation with Michael Douglas on the set of *Wall Street* over "lousy acting" in the film's first two scenes. Stone confirmed that he had, indeed, challenged Douglas. "He just wasn't giving me what I wanted and by shocking him with criticism he went into a retreat. Then he came back the next day or two days later and I tell you there was a tremendous difference in the man. He was on the money. He was angry, he was angry at me, but it was a good anger that he took out on me and I tell you there was a tremendous difference the third day as opposed to the first day. . . . Sometimes confrontation, if it's done well, can be a shock, and a shock can be a stimulus to change."[2]

What's made all of Stone's films so controversial, however, and really fabulous material for heated debate, is the moral battles waged in each of his movies. Many of these are battles so heated that some people leave the theater dismissing Stone as a zealot, his movies as unbalanced passion plays or heavy-handed morality tales. His characters, after all, are often archetypes of the "dark" villains and "light" heroes of fables.

In *Wall Street*, those characters are of course the evil Gekko in battle with altruistic Carl Fox, Bud's father (Martin Sheen). Add to this the familiar character of the old "seer," in this case Lou Mannheim (Hal Holbrook), Bud's senior colleague. As in many of Stone's movies, these central characters periodically step forward to summarize their positions and values in the broad strokes of, say, melodrama.

With all these opposing forces at work, people start wondering, what side is Stone really *on*? Is he *against* violence or *indulging* it in *Natural Born Killers*? In *Wall Street*, is he taking the stance of a liberal fighting against capitalist value systems or is he as disgusted by righteous liberalism as by the "goods" mentality the film so openly condemns?

The answers, of course, are irrelevant unless you're into writing profiles of Hollywood personalities. What *is* relevant is that Stone's movies force you to consider morally complex worlds, and these make you—if you're really on your toes—position yourself and your own values in ethical relation to the characters in his films.

No challenge could be more productive for someone training for success. Success, Stone's *Wall Street* proposes, has got to include the parameters of decency, or why even bother? But what exactly are those parameters?

The kind of critical, evaluative thinking that *Wall Street* stimulates for its viewers may just give you an occasion for the sort of moral self-evaluation and recognition of personal beliefs that should never go neglected as you muster your absolute powers.

Gordon Gekko, with his dark morality and his glitzy, high-gloss, nouveau-art-infested lair, may appear at first to be a reptilian cousin to the spoiled, narcissistic Charlie Kane, a familiar cautionary figure; but Gekko has never deluded himself into thinking he has any interest in helping others. His interest in cutthroat, high-stakes gambling well surpasses his interest in money, and with none of Kane's "generous" posturing.

Why wreck a promising company and its staff? "Because it's wreckable," Gekko remarks candidly and with an obvious thrill. He's openly disinterested in feelings, and encourages others to abandon theirs if they want to get ahead. Unlike Kane, too, Gekko's interests seem to blend in neatly with the interests and visions of most everyone else around him. Gordon Gekko's vision statement, his personal Declaration of Principles? *Greed is good.*

The story here is fairly straightforward—the seduction of a fresh-faced, naive young kid by a corrupt and rascally corporate predator. Bud dreams of money, power, luxury, stature, and reputation, all of which he thinks he'll find in the Big Leagues with the millionaire trader who is his hero. Bud's not just interested in doing business with Gekko, he's interested in finding a mentor who'll teach him how to move at the highest levels, and to shake himself free of the burdensome ethics of his union-organizer father, who encourages Bud to work at helping others and to earn money the "hard way"—as he puts it, by "*creating*" not off "the buying and selling of others." Gekko's credo, on the other hand? "I create nothing. I own."

This conflict of mentoring visions creates a human side to *Wall Street* and turns a film that everybody expected to be a yawn into pathetic tragedy. There's not just illegal dealmaking going on here. There's a story of dueling mentors, as Gekko teaches Bud how to be a manipulator while Bud's father, an aircraft mechanic from Queens, tries to get him to be a man who uses his honor, not his bank book, as credentials.

The result is a Faustian tug of war in which Fox first sells his soul to Gekko for a piece of the action; an artsy girlfriend, Darien Taylor (Daryl Hannah), who knows the difference between cubism and dada and who shares Bud's lust for money; and an overdecorated co-op on the East Side. He is then transformed and brought to a dead halt by the arrival of the boys from the SEC. He's frisked and handcuffed and led from his big new office by federal agents. In the end, the prodigal son tearfully seeks redemption from his father.

The movie takes you on an exhaustive tour through the various phases of Bud's surrender to greed as he acquires his fancy lifestyle and endless gadgets for making meals too good-looking to eat. In fact, this seems to be an apt metaphor for the world Bud covets, where look is sustenance enough. Bud's chic girlfriend is appalled that his apartment has real brick walls—but when Bud moves to the East Side, she wallpapers his place in faux brick that is apparently a better "look" than the real thing. And she herself is all hats and hair and backless dresses, with little else to offer.

You also witness Bud's inevitable break with Carl Fox (these scenes between real-life father and son Martin and Charlie Sheen vibrate with genuine feeling), as well as his eventual assault on the corrupt mentor Gekko, who demands that Bud turn—lethally and indifferently—on his own father. Using all the ruthless techniques Gekko has taught him, Bud goes after Gekko, this time using deceit in the name of decency. His father, and the others whose jobs are saved at the airline Bud rescues from Gekko's grip, assure Bud that he did the right thing, reminding him of all the good that his attack on Gekko will bring.

The film clearly reveals Wall Street's tectonic shift from decency to deals by the way these characters speak, unearthing volumes about how they think and what they value, opening up their souls for anyone within hearing distance. Their words, expressions, sentences—all signal to others the truth within them. All a viewer needs is a bit of the semanticist's power of observation and the ability to decode how these characters make references to things and ideas.

Instantly, we possess a lavish dossier on their inner selves. Consider, for example, several verbal revelations from Gekko:

To another dealmaker:

If it looks as good as on paper, we're in the kill zone, pal. We can lock and load. Lunch? Ah, you gotta be kiddin', lunch is for wimps.

To Bud Fox:

Give me guys that are poor, smart, and hungry and no feelings. Win a few, lose a few, but you keep on fighting. And if you need a friend, get a dog. It's trench warfare out there, pal.

And, to the stockholders of a company he is trying to take over:

> I am not a destroyer of companies. I am a liberator of them. The point is, ladies and gentlemen, that greed, for lack of a better word, is good.

This guy is for real. So real that it comes as no surprise to his colleagues that, seconds after his paean to avarice, this deal-maker, corporate raider, speculator, arbitrageur extraordinaire, and one of the highest rollers on Wall Street, mugs at them as if to say, "Words are merely moves in the game." Gekko, it turns out, is the kind of person who would have been on the A-list for junk bond king Michael Milken's "Predators' Ball," Drexel-Burnham's annual clients' conference held at a posh hotel in Beverly Hills. He would have been right at home. His tastes run to steak tartare at exclusive restaurants, a trophy wife, stretch limos, ghastly modern art, and a to-die-for house in the Hamptons.

Gekko is a gecko, a cold-blooded lizard that has a nasty bite and sheds its tail when trapped. He makes his money primarily by illegally obtaining insider information on takeover deals. He's an "Arb" who gambles on securities of firms that are the subject of possible takeovers. He makes zillions by profiting from the difference between their purchase price and the selling price when the transaction takes place. He's mastered the art of buying low and selling high.

But there's something wrong here. Gekko—whose character is loosely based on Ivan Boesky, the real-life, pink-Rolls-Roycedriving archcriminal of the age of avarice—twists language as ruthlessly as he twists people, for his own gain. Boesky, an admitted "money-oriented monomaniac," was called "Ivan the Terrible" by his Wall Street cronies, which tells you everything you need to know about his reputation. This one-time genius at risk arbitrage who lived extravagantly and liked to throw $500-a-plate dinner parties at the Plaza, after being convicted by the zealous then–U.S. District Attorney Rudolph Giuliani, went on to a kinder and gentler lifestyle, pursuing rabbinical studies and doing good works for any homeless people who would have anything to do with him.

Gekko's lair, as steely as his language and his values, is an elegant office suite overlooking everything important in Manhattan, full of telephone consoles with scores of buttons and video screens streaming with stock and bond market figures. His network is extensive; he's king of the Rolodex without the Rolodex—he has a girl for that—taking three conference calls at once and paying no attention to one of his secretaries when she informs him that his wife is waiting on the phone.

His modus operandi is simple. Tap into a sufficiently large network of informants so that the Securities and Exchange Commission cannot link him to any one source. Recruit young Turks who buy into the argument that insider trading is OK because "everybody's doing it." Run dirty trades through secret offshore banks. Retain prominent investment houses that do business through these banks. Recruit law firms that, for a little cooperation, will make tens of millions in a few weeks on a deal.

It's a way to make a buck.

Just consider the possibilities. Bumblewitz Mining is all set to acquire Hopvest Extraction, another mining outfit. As usual, vague rumors fly the day before the deal is consummated. But, in fact, the buzz about the Bumblewitz deal started days earlier when trading in its shares was six times the previous week's daily average. Bumblewitz shares, which had been holding fairly steady at $80, jumped by 12 percent a week before the deal and 9.5 percent several days earlier, when the Dow Jones industrial average happened to fall. At the same time, trading in options on Bumblewitz shares started spiking several days before the deal was made public. Quite obviously, piles of profits have been made with privileged information. But, if the SEC spots these unusual trading patterns, you're cooked.

On the other side of this risky, thrill-a-minute spectrum is Carl Fox, a guy whose language and manner manifest all his values and emotional ties to others. His focus is on unions, coalitions of people, and on plain, as-you-feel-it speech. Here's a typical Carl Fox perspective:

> CARL    The rich have been doing it to the poor since the beginning of time. The only difference between the pyramids and the Empire State Building is the Egyptians didn't allow unions. I know what this guy is all about. Greed. He don't give a damn about Blue Star or the unions. He's in and out for the buck, and he don't take prisoners.

A far cry from Gekko's glib war yodeling. And then there's that other, free-floating perspective of office sage Lou

Mannheim, who passes through the offices of Bud's firm as a sort of Greek chorus, dispensing pointers from what sounds like some ancient moral tip sheet on how to survive Wall Street trading. Mannheim's language sounds antique, nearly loony, as he encourages Bud to move slowly and to stare into the "abyss" to "find himself." Mannheim—and Bud's father—believe, apparently, in what sounds like a bygone era when morality could be established and maintained through an organized list of behaviors and spot-checks that recognize few of the ambiguities of the changing business age they live in.

What's a guy like Bud—a tabula rasa—to do, surrounded by so many opposing forces? His initial position—that he has a pathetic dependence on his father's wallet, and a better opportunity for a richer life—seems well taken. If it's possible to make money fast without breaking your back, why not learn how to do that? Makes sense.

The problem that Bud encounters is that "fast"—the kind of "fast" that has made Gekko his millions—seems in this tale to mean bending a few rules. Or breaking a few laws. And the moral discomfort Bud obviously feels at first after betraying his father's confidence to win Gekko's attention is, well, just damned inconvenient. That inconvenience sets him on his course of legitimizing his choices, no matter how illegal or money-hungry they become.

Bud has no moral barometer of his own, and is quite willing to accept the idea that he does not need one because "everybody does it." Because he has never bothered to define his own belief system, he's a sponge for the aggressive, glittering ideas

Gekko foists upon him. Unfortunately, Bud has also never learned, like Gekko, to consider the power and purpose of language, and is unable to comprehend the meaning of the words he hears.

This poor kid still hasn't found a language of his own, to express his own identity. He often confuses definitions, and he's a sap for Gekko's greed speech. Of course, as soon as the words "greed is good" are out of Gekko's mouth, you just know they're wrong. But Bud is wowed, and this naturally is proof that he has been fully seduced by his mentor. He has become Gekko's perfect pawn, and it is not until Gekko's various impersonal crimes take on a personal tone that Bud wakes up to the truth about Gekko.

In turning on Gekko, Bud has apparently used a "triage" system in which he evaluates for himself which situation is worse than another and—with no good situations to choose from—selects the one he finds least morally disturbing. He is confronted with a situation that he cannot justify—the total destruction of his father's career and company. He's watched Gekko's sharklike maneuvers before, but when it's his own father at stake? Forget it. This is the mirror Bud has needed. Although Bud has earlier blamed his father for "triaging"— choosing his "men" over his son—Bud chooses to rely on this same system to define a fuzzy moral parameter for himself. The ending, then, seems fairly resolved as Bud—who appears never to have gone past the stage of mere moral relativism—heads for court, and Carl Fox delivers this final philosophical package: "Maybe in some kind of screwed up way it's the best thing that could have happened to you. Stop going for the easy buck and produce something with your life." Bud's crimes in the name of decency are forgivable. Crimes in the name of greed are not.

But . . . do you believe that?

What's great about Stone's movies is that these seemingly "pat" conclusions to his morality plays are really provoking larger ideas. It's quite clear that criminal behavior to make lots of money is wrong; but what if you're earning hand over fist, like Gekko, and never break the law at all? To ask yourself, Is that OK? seems a question too dumb to answer. Sure! Wait . . . *Wall Street* suggests that there's got to be some sort of out-reaching reason for making money that focuses not on goods but on people. Create, don't own. Evaluate your motives. Straighten up and fly right. Save an airline. There's got to be a clear humanistic goal.

But . . . do you believe *that*?

Of course, Bud's father claims to believe that. So does Lou Mannheim, who trusts in sound ethics manifested by a slow pace. Still, Carl Fox is self-righteous there at the end, ready to justify the means by the end in the grand style of an overzeal-ous liberal pointing fingers at the rich guys. If Carl Fox were the extraordinary moral leader his son takes him to be by the end of this movie—and Bud switches quickly from Gekko postures to the more swaggering stance, walk, and cigarette-smoking gestures of his father—he would probably recognize that who the victim *is* doesn't necessarily justify the crime.

But . . . do you believe *that*?

*Wall Street* asks questions of you that demand you take stances, make arguments, persuade your colleagues, collect information, review the materials, and interpret the data you have been given to lead yourself to a committed position. This is one movie you can't just watch for tips and illustrations. Rest assured that when a movie is wrapped up neatly like this one, there's probably something tremendous beneath the surface— a large, critical issue, conceived and pondered by the director, that a good leader shouldn't neglect to study and explore.

What *Wall Street* demands to know is, What are *your* moral parameters? On what do you wish to base them? You won't find the answer to that question in the latest guidebook on ethics in management or at a two-day corporate retreat. And if you look for a leader to follow in this film, you probably won't find one. No doubt you've disqualified that insect-eating monomaniac Gekko as a sound leader for his young protégé Bud. Gekko's charisma and ego and greed—made crystal-clear when he asks Bud to "Astonish me, pal. New info. I don't care where or how you get it."—can't possibly be mistaken for leadership. Nor is he mentoring. He's controlling. Sure, he may, like his role model Ivan Boesky, ultimately find atonement in prison, good works, and rabbinical studies, but for now who'd want to own *that* junk bond?

Bud Fox may have had a limping sort of epiphany at the end of *Wall Street* that may redeem him sooner or later (his lonely walk into federal court as a defendant rivets your attention) but that hardly qualifies him for the mantle of leadership, at least for now. He is, though, riding the moral roller coaster that seems to have always thrilled boomers, yuppies, X-ers, and Net-Gens, and he'll no doubt face more exhilarating ascents and terrifying plunges before this journey is over.

Social scientists who study the process of moral development would view Bud's case as quite normal. People move through a succession of three stages. At first what is right is fixed—defined by parents, teachers, religious leaders, and others. They rely on these authority figures and their "thou shalt nots." The second stage provides few guidelines and constraints. Here morality becomes relative, an infinity of individual viewpoints—a stage that enables Bud to rationalize his very illegal activities on behalf of Gekko. Finally, in the third stage, people acquire a sense of themselves as free and autonomous human beings; they make moral and ethical decisions not based on others' authority or on relativistic calculation. Instead they make decisions about what is right and what is wrong after weighing evidence from multiple sources. Some people reach this third stage when they are well into adulthood. Others never reach it. As Claudia Harris and William Brown, who have plumbed *Wall Street* for its moral lessons, point out, it is clear that Bud Fox remains firmly in the second stage at the end of the film.[3] Surely leadership must have a moral component, and that quality is as yet lacking in him.

And what about Lou Mannheim, the aging statesman of the firm, whose "stick to the fundamentals" lecture to Bud makes so much sense? You can disqualify old war horse Lou too, an out-of-it preacher who cannot reach the young man he worries over because he never really tries.

What about Carl Fox, Bud's stolid and blue-collar father, whose conservative values and pro-worker bent seem somehow noble? His lectures, like Mannheim's, helpfully invoke what leadership guru Stephen Covey calls the law of the farm: "You must prepare the ground, put in the seed, cultivate it, weed it, water it, then gradually nurture growth and development to full maturity."[4] Too bad that both Carl and Lou are ultimately shown to be ineffectual persuaders whose messages about good moral and economic behavior slip by their target. As mentors, they're both severely challenged. It's too bad that Carl's odd righteousness—his inability to recognize that everyone's down there in the dirt, even himself—makes him seem a bit suspect.

If you believe, as we do, that leadership is "an influence relationship among leaders and followers who intend real changes that reflect their mutual purposes,"[5] then you are driven, by simple logic, to an inescapable conclusion. The leader "in" *Wall Street* is not *in* the movie. What to do?

Well, start by doing what *Wall Street* asks you to do: think about the important difference between law and morality. Yes, some have called Oliver Stone a social revolutionary, an America hater, a champion of disinformation, a thrower of cultural cannonballs, a revisionist. But in *Wall Street* Stone does provoke intellectual discourse about the possibility that "business ethics" is, and always will be, an oxymoron that has as much to do with personal choices as with obvious legalities. He has gotten us to consider whether Adam Smith was right when he argued in *An Inquiry into the Nature and Causes of the Wealth of Nations* that "self-interest" is good, that every individual in pursuing his or her own good is led, as if by an invisible hand, to achieve the best good for all. It's a flexible notion that leaves room for a lot of errors. Is the idea even operable these days?

Recent studies have confirmed what most of us suspect. A 1994 Gallup poll, for example, revealed that only the government ranks lower than corporations in trustworthiness. And a 1996 study done at Tulane University found that two out of every five controllers and nearly half of all top executives were willing to commit fraud in role-playing exercises. A whopping 87 percent made at least one fraudulent decision in the course of simulated work situations.

What about ordinary workers? The news is not good. Almost half admitted to unethical actions within the past year—cutting corners on quality, covering up incidents, abusing or lying about sick days, deceiving customers, lying to a supervisor or underling, and taking credit for a colleague's ideas. No wonder one expert has, after years of study, concluded that "ethics is a broad and often murky area."[6] Apparently so. One company, in desperation, has even launched an ethics-training program using a board game called "The Ethics Challenge," which presents its players with a wide array of ethics issues featuring characters from the "Dilbert" cartoon strip.

But to whom should you turn now, as you contemplate these moral questions? Stone, it seems, has attempted to give you your *self*, by diving back and forth in *Wall Street* between the opposing forces that propel every human being toward success and toward helping others to succeed.

There's no denying, the parameters of our moral worlds are ambiguous, difficult to navigate, and—certainly in *Wall Street* though not necessarily in our lives—without sound leaders.

Who's left?

You are.

# ENDNOTES

CHAPTER ONE

**Following Your Hunch: *The Hunt for Red October***

1. Quinn Spitzer and Ron Evans, "The New Business Leader: Socrates with a Baton," *Strategy & Leadership* 5, no. 25 (1997): 32.

2. Marcia Yudkin, "Are You Intuitive?" *Natural Health* 24, no. 3 (1994): 70.

3. Gretchen Vogel, "Scientists Probe Feelings Behind Decision Making," *Science* 275 (1997): 1269.

4. Daniel Cappon, "A New Approach to Intuition: IQ2," *Omni* 16, no. 12 (1994): 34.

5. Stan Davis, "Rumble, Rumble," *Training & Development* 50, no. 11 (1996): 44.

6. Spitzer and Evans.

7. Daniel Cappon, "The Anatomy of Intuition," *Psychology Today* 26, no. 3 (1993): 40.

CHAPTER TWO

The Importance of Improvisation: *Apollo 13*

1. Richard Corliss, "Hell of a Ride," *Time,* 3 July 1995, p. 50.

2. Charles Murray and Catherine Bly Cox, *Apollo: The Race to the Moon* (New York: Simon & Schuster, 1989), p. 162.

3. Mary M. Crossan, Roderick E. White, Henry W. Lane, and Leo Klus, "The Improvising Organization: Where Planning Meets Opportunity," *Organizational Dynamics* (Spring 1996):20.


CHAPTER THREE

The Failed Promise of Heroic Leadership: *Dead Poets Society*

1. Michael Porter, "Creating Tomorrow's Advantages," in *Rethinking the Future: Business, Principles, Competition, Control, Leadership, Markets and the World,* ed. Rowan Gibson (London: Nicholas Brealey, 1997), p. 39.

2. Desson Howe, "*Dead Poets Society*: Mr. Williams's English Lit," *Washington Post,* 9 June 1989, Weekend, p. 43.

3. Noel M. Tichy and Stratford Sherman, *Control Your Destiny or Someone Else Will: Lessons in Mastering Change—the Principles Jack Welch Is Using to Revolutionize General Electric* (New York: HarperBusiness, 1994), p. 239.

4. Robert B. Heilman, "The Great Teacher Myth," *The American Scholar* 60:3 (1991):418.

5. Ibid, p. 423.

CHAPTER FOUR

**Turning Around a Faltering Team:** *Hoosiers*

1. William Gildea, *Where the Game Matters Most* (New York: Little, Brown, 1997), p. 3.

2. Joel Kotkin, *How Race, Religion, and Identity Determine Success in the New Global Economy* (New York: Random House, 1992), p. 18.

3. William H. Gass, "Exile," in *Best American Essays*, ed. Susan Sontag (New York: Ticknor and Fields, 1992), p. 126.

4. Ralph T. King, Jr., "Jeans Therapy: Levi's Factory Workers Are Assigned to Teams, and Morale Takes a Hit," *Asia Wall Street Journal*, 26 May 1998, p. 1.

5. B. M. Bass and B. J. Avolio, "The Implications of Transactional and Transformational Leadership for Individual, Team, and Organizational Development," *Research in Organizational Change and Development* 4 (1990): 231–272.

CHAPTER FIVE

**Mentors and Protégés:** *Norma Rae*

1. Don Tapscott, "Minds Over Matter," *Business 2.0*, January 1999, p. 89.

2. W. F. Foster, "Toward a Critical Practice of Leadership," in *Critical Perspectives on Educational Leadership*, ed. J. Smyth (London: Falmer, 1992), p. 46.

3. Denis Boyles, "Find Your Guide: Self-Employed and Seeking a Mentor," *Success*, July 1998, p. 20.

4. Terri A. Scandura, "Dysfunctional Mentoring Relationships and Outcomes," *Journal of Management*, 1 May 1998, p. 449.

5. Hal Lancaster, "How Women Can Find Mentors in a World with Few Male Role Models," *Wall Street Journal*, 1 April 1997, p. B1.

6. Scandura.


CHAPTER SIX

**Socratic Leadership: *12 Angry Men***

1. Jonathan E. Adler, "Open Minds and the Argument from Ignorance," *Skeptical Inquirer*, 11 January 1998, p. 41.

2. Hendrick, Hal W. "Perceptual Accuracy of Self and Others and Leadership Status" in *Measures of Leadership*, eds. Kenneth Clark and Miriam Clark (West Orange, N.J.: Leadership Library of America, 1990), p. 511.

3. Leonard Grob, "The Socratic Model," in *Leadership: Multidisciplinary Perspectives*, ed. Barbara Kellerman (Englewood Cliffs, N.J.: Prentice-Hall, 1984), p. 263.

4. Shari Caudron, "Keeping Team Conflict Alive," *Training & Development*, 9 September 1998, p. 48.

5. Jay Boyer, *Sidney Lumet, Twayne's Filmmaker Series VI* (New York: Twayne Publishers, 1993), p. 27.


CHAPTER SEVEN

**Turning Around a Troubled Organization:**
***Twelve O'Clock High***

1. The Center for Leadership Studies, promotional brochure (Rancho Bernardo, Calif., 1997).

2. Robert H. Miles, *Orientation for Viewing* Twelve O'Clock High (Boston: Harvard Business School Publishing, 1995).

3. John Keegan, *The Mask of Command* (New York: Penguin USA, 1989), p. 213.

4. Jan P. Muczyk and Robert P. Steel, "Leadership Style and the Turnaround Executive," *Business Horizons,* 3 March 1998, p. 39.
5. Ibid.
6. Mike Johnson, "Taking the Lid Off Leadership," *Management Review* 85, no. 11 (1996): 59.
7. Rebecca Blumenstein, "A New CEO's Choice: Keep the Old Team or Bring in Your Own," *Wall Street Journal,* 24 December 1998, p. A1.
8. Gillian Flynn, "A Flight Plan for Success," *Workforce,* July 1997, p. 72.

CHAPTER EIGHT
**When Leadership Fails: *Citizen Kane***
1. Louis Giannetti, *Understanding Movies* (Englewood Cliffs, N.J.: Prentice Hall, 1987), p. 428.
2. Bob Stephens, "Welles Masterpiece Back in Fresh Print," *San Francisco Examiner,* 2 October 1998, p. C3.
3. Manfred F. R. Kets de Vries, "The Dark Side of Entrepreneurship," *Harvard Business Review,* November-December 1985, p. 160.
4. F. Scott Fizgerald, *The Crack Up* (New York, New Directions, 1956), p. 69.
5. James Krohe, Jr., "Do You Really Need a Mission Statement?" *Across the Board,* July-August 1995, p. 16.
6. Richard Kramer and Thomas Lennon, "The Battle Over *Citizen Kane,*" *The American Experience,* 1996, documentary directed by Michael Epstein and Thomas Lennon, Lennon Documentary Group.

7. John Tebbel, *The Life and Good Times of William Randolph Hearst* (New York: E. P. Dutton, 1952), p. 373.

8. David C. McClellan and David H. Burnham, "Power Is the Great Motivator," *Harvard Business Review*, January-February 1995, p. 2.

9. Ichak Adizes, *The Pursuit of Prime: Maximize Your Company's Success* (Knowledge Exchange, 1997), p. 16.

10. Simon Callow, *Orson Welles: The Road to Xanadu* (New York: Penguin Books, 1995), p. 485.

11. Kramer and Lennon.

CHAPTER NINE

**Morality and Leadership: *Wall Street***

1. Marita Sturken, "Reenactment, Fantasy, and the Paranoia of History: Oliver Stone's Docudramas," *History and Theory*, December 1997, p. 64.

2. Stuart Fischoff, "Oliver Stone," *Psychology Today* 26, no. 5 (1993): 44.

3. Claudia Harris and William Brown, *Teaching Notes for* Wall Street, *Hartwick Classic Leadership Case* (New York: Hartwick, 1996), p. 6.

4. Stephen R. Covey, *Principle-Centered Leadership* (New York: Simon & Schuster, 1992), p. 161.

5. Joseph C. Rost, Leadership for the Twenty-First Century (New York: Praeger, 1991), p. 102.

6. Samuel Greengard, "50% of Your Employees Are Lying, Cheating & Stealing," *Workforce*, October 1997, p. 53.

# BIBLIOGRAPHY

Allen, Robert C, and Douglas Gomery. *Film History: Theory and Practice.* New York: Alfred A. Knopf, 1985.

Battcock, Gregory. *The New American Cinema: A Critical Anthology.* New York: E. P. Dutton, 1967.

Barzin, André. *Orson Welles: A Critical View.* New York: Harper & Row, 1978.

———. *What Is Cinema?* Berkeley: University of California Press, 1967.

Beja, Morris. *Film and Literature.* New York: Longman, 1979.

Belton, John. *Movies and Mass Culture.* New Brunswick, N.J.: Rutgers University Press, 1996.

Bergan, Ronald. *Francis Ford Coppola: Close Up the Making of His Movies.* New York: Thunder's Mouth Press, 1998.

Bergman, Paul, and Michael Asimow. *Reel Justice: The Courtroom Goes to the Movies.* Kansas City, Mo.: Andrews McMeel Publishing, 1996.

Blockbuster Entertainment. *Blockbuster Entertainment Guide to Movies and Videos 1998.* New York: Dell Books, 1997.

Boorstin, Jon. *Making Movies Work: Thinking Like a Filmmaker.* Beverly Hills, Calif.: Silman-James Press, 1995.

Bordwell, David, Janet Staiger, and Kristin Thompson. *The Classical Hollywood Cinema: Film Style and Mode of Production to 1960.* New York: Columbia University Press, 1985.

Carnes, Mark C., Ted Mico, and John Miller-Monzon. *Past Imperfect: History According to the Movies.* Brooklyn, N.Y.: Owlet, 1996.

Carringer, Robert L. *The Making of* Citizen Kane. Berkeley: University of California Press, 1985.

Cendrars, Blaise, Jean Guerin, and Garrett White. *Hollywood: Mecca of the Movies.* Berkeley: University of California Press, 1995.

Condon, Thomas. *The Enneagram Movie and Video Guide: How to See Personality Styles in the Movies.* Bend, Oreg.: Changeworks, 1994.

Corey, Melinda, and George Ochoa. *The Dictionary of Film Quotations: 6,000 Provocative Movie Quotes from 1,000 Movies.* New York: Crown Publishers, 1995.

Denver, John, ed. *Legal Reelism: Movies as Legal Texts.* Champaign-Urbana: University of Illinois Press, 1996.

Ebert, Roger, and Gene Siskel. *The Future of the Movies: Interviews with Martin Scorsese, Steven Spielberg, and George Lucas.* Kansas City, Mo.: Andrews McMeel Publishing, 1991.

Entertainment Weekly. *The "Entertainment Weekly" Guide to the Greatest Movies Ever Made.* New York: Warner Books, 1994.

Fitzgerald, F. Scott. *The Crack Up.* New York: New Directions Press, 1956.

Gabler, Neal. *Life, the Movie: How Entertainment Conquered Reality*. New York: Alfred A. Knopf, 1998.

Gass, William H. "Exile," in *Best American Essays*, ed. Susan Sontag. New York: Ticknor and Fields, 1992.

Gianetti, Louis. *Understanding Movies*. Englewood Cliffs, N.J.: Prentice-Hall, 1987.

Gilmore, Michael T. *Differences in the Dark: American Movies and English Theater*. New York: Columbia University Press, 1998.

Goldstein, Laurence, and Ira Konigsberg. *The Movies: Texts, Receptions, Exposures*. Ann Arbor, Mich.: University of Michigan Press, 1991.

Guttmacher, Peter. *Legendary War Movies*. New York: Metro Books, 1996.

Haskell, Molly. *From Reverence to Rape: The Treatment of Women in the Movies*. Chicago: The University of Chicago Press, 1987.

Hitzeroth, Deborah, and Sharon Heerboth. *Movies: The World on Film (The Encyclopedia of Discovery and Invention)*. San Diego, Calif.: Lucent Books, 1991.

Hurt, James. *Focus on Film and Theatre*. Englewood Cliffs, N.J.: Prentice-Hall, 1975.

Issari, M. Ali. *Cinema Verite*. East Lansing: Michigan State University Press, 1971.

Kael, Pauline. *Nights at the Movies: Expanded for the 90s with 800 New Reviews*. New York: Henry Holt and Co., 1991.

Kirkham, Pat, and Janet Thumin. *Me Jane: Masculinity, Movies and Women*. New York: St. Martin's Press, 1995.

Lasky, Betty. *RKO: The Biggest Little Major of Them All*. Englewood Cliffs, N.J.: Prentice-Hall, 1984.

Lovell, Alan, and Jim Hillier. *Studies in Documentary.* New York: Viking, 1972.

Lumet, Sidney. *Making Movies.* New York: Vintage Books, 1996.

MacBean, James Roy. *Film and Revolution.* Bloomington: Indiana University Press, 1975.

Marsh, Clive, and Gaye Ortiz. *Explorations in Theology and Film: Movies and Meaning.* Malden, Mass.: Blackwell Publishers, 1998.

McAuliff, Jody. *Plays, Movies, and Critics.* Durham, N.C.: Duke University Press, 1993.

McDougal, Stuart Y. *Made into Movies: From Literature to Film.* New York: Holt Rinehart & Winston, 1997.

Nicoll, Allardyce. *Film and Theatre.* New York: Crowell, 1936.

Nilsen, Vladimir. *The Cinema as a Graphic Art.* New York: Hill and Wang, 1959.

Norden, Martin F. *The Cinema of Isolation: A History of Physical Disability in the Movies.* New Brunswick, N.J.: Rutgers University Press, 1994.

O'Brien, Geoffrey. *The Phantom Empire: Movies in the Mind of the Twentieth Century.* New York: W. W. Norton & Co., 1995.

O'Brien, Lisa, and Stephen MacEachern. *Lights, Camera, Action! Making Movies and TV from the Inside Out.* Forestville: Owl Communications, 1998.

Perkins, V. F., and Foster Hirsch. *Film as Film: Understanding and Judging Movies.* New York: Da Capo Press, 1993.

Perry, George C. *Steven Spielberg: Close Up the Making of His Movies.* New York: Thunder's Mouth Press, 1998.

Prince, Stephen. *Movies and Meaning: An Introduction to Film.* Needham Heights, Mass.: Allyn & Bacon, 1996.

Proctor, Russell F., II. *Communication in Film.* Orlando, Fla.: Harcourt Brace & Company, 1996.

Roberts, Ken. *The Hollywood Principle.* Ojai, Calif.: Four Star Publishing, 1991.

Rosenbaum, Jonathan. *Movies as Politics.* Berkeley: University of California Press, 1997.

Rosenbaum, Jonathan. *Placing Movies: The Practice of Film Criticism.* Berkeley: University of California Press, 1995.

Rossell, Deac. *Living Pictures: The Origins of the Movies.* Albany, N.Y.: State University of New York Press, 1998.

Schanzer, Karl, and Thomas Lee Wright. *American Screenwriters: The Insider's Look at the Art, the Craft, and the Business of Writing Movies.* New York: Avon Books, 1993.

Schell, Terri. *The Video Source Book: A Guide to Programs Currently Available on Video in the Areas of: Movies/Entertainment, General Interest/Education, Sports.* Detroit, Mich.: Gale Research, 1998.

Scorsese, Martin, Michael Henry Wilson, and British Film Institute. *A Personal Journey with Martin Scorsese Through American Movies.* New York: Hyperion, 1997.

Seger, Linda, and Whetmore, Edward Jay. *From Script to Screen: The Collaborative Art of Film Making.* New York: Henry Holt and Co., 1994.

Sinyard, Neil. *Silent Movies.* New York: Mithmark, 1994.

Stauffacher, Frank. *Art in Cinema.* New York: Arno Press, 1969.

Tudor, Andrew. *Theories of Film.* New York: Viking, 1974.

Tyler, Parker. *Magic and Myth of the Movies.* New York: Simon and Schuster, 1944.

Wakoski, Diane. *Argonaut Rose: Archaeology of Movies and Books,* vol. 4. Santa Rosa, Calif.: Black Sparrow Press, 1998.

Wilson, John Morgan. *Inside Hollywood: A Writer's Guide to Researching the World of Movies and TV.* Cincinnati, Oh.: Writers Digest Books, 1998.

Youngblood, Gene. *Expanded Cinema.* New York: E. P. Dutton, 1970.

Zaniello, Tom. *Working Stiffs, Union Maids, Reds, and Riffraff: An Organized Guide to Films About Labor.* Ithaca, N.Y.: Cornell University Press, 1996.

# INDEX

221